Dedicated to Sherry, Lynn and all the volunteers of the Ben Nobleman Park Community Orchard.

Growing Urban Orchards:
The Ups, Downs and How-tos of Fruit Tree Care in the City
By Susan Poizner

Illustrations: Sherry Firing
Copy Editors: Jack Kirchhoff, Lynn Nicholas
Design: Bungalow

Publisher:
Orchard People (2359434 Ontario Inc.):
107 Everden Road,
Toronto, ON M6C 3K7
Canada
www.urbanfruittree.com

All rights reserved. No part of this book may be reproduced or transmitted in any form or by any means, electronic or mechanical, including photocopying, recording or by any information storage and retrieval system, without written permission from the author, except for the inclusion of brief quotations in a review.

Copyright: 2014 Orchard People (2359434 Ontario Inc.):
First Edition, 2014

Published in Canada

Growing Urban Orchards

The Ups, Downs and How-tos of Fruit Tree Care in the City

By Susan Poizner

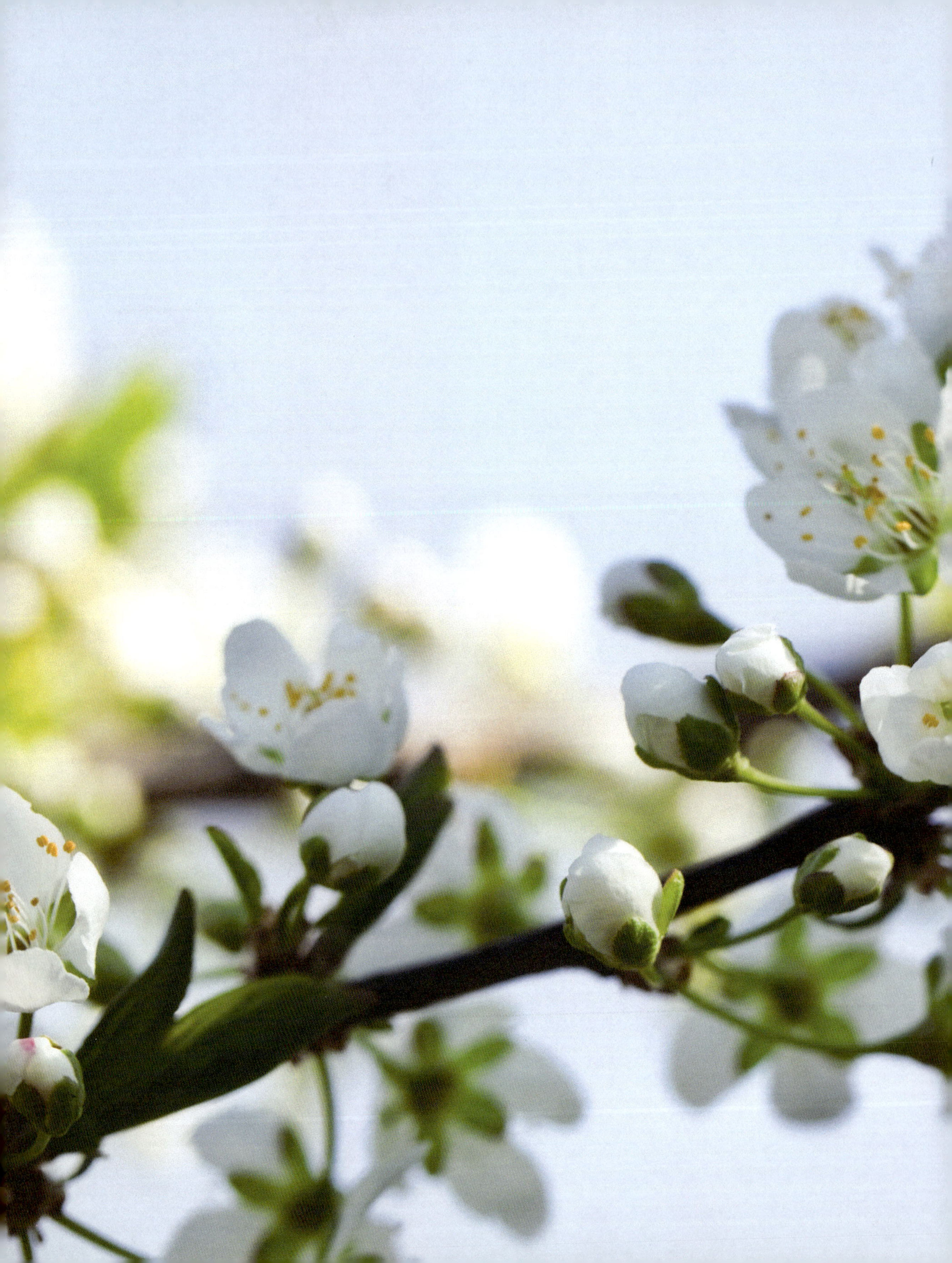

Growing Urban Orchards

The Ups, Downs and How-tos of Fruit Tree Care in the City

By Susan Poizner

GROWING URBAN ORCHARDS

Table of Contents

Part 1: Introduction

Chapter 1: Discovering Urban Orchards — 3

Chapter 2: Selecting Your Site — 7

Site Preparation — 8
Orchard Inspiration: Walnut Way, Milwaukee, WI — 10

Chapter 3: Parts of a Fruit Tree — 13
Blossoms and Fruit — 13
Buds and Leaves — 16
Roots — 18
Trunk and Bark — 20
The Grafted Tree — 22
Understanding Grafting:
The Story of the McIntosh Apple — 23

Part 2: Selecting, Planting and Caring for Your Tree

Chapter 4: Selecting Your Fruit Trees — 25

Hardiness — 26
Disease Resistance — 26
Tree Size — 27
Cross-Pollinating Fruit Trees — 27
Self-Pollinating Fruit Trees — 27
Staggering the Harvest — 28
Eating, Cooking or Canning — 28
Heirloom Trees — 28
Orchard Inspiration:
Community Orchard Research Project, Calgary, AB. — 30
Native Trees — 31
Nut Trees — 31
Ordering Trees in the Fall for Spring — 31
Bare Root Versus Potted Trees — 32
Inspecting Your New Tree — 32
Types of Fruit — 33

Chapter 5: Planting Your Tree — 35

Planting a Bare Root Tree — 36
"Whipping" the Tree — 38
Staking a Tree — 38
Planting a Potted Tree — 39

Chapter 6: Caring for Your Tree — 41

Young Tree Care — 42
Watering — 42
Feeding — 44
Mulching — 44

Removing the Baby Fruit	44
Pruning	44
Weeding	45
Mouse Guards	45
Mature Tree Care	45
Irrigation for Older Trees	45
Thinning the Fruit for Older Trees	45
Orchard Inspiration: The Sharing Farm Society, Richmond, BC	47

Part 3: Feeding, Pruning and Protecting Your Tree

Chapter 7: Feeding Your Trees — 49

What is Soil?	50
Assessing Your Soil	51
Soil Texture	51
Soil pH and Nutrients	51
Orchard Inspiration: Strathcona Community Garden, Vancouver, BC	52
N-P-K Labels	54
Mulching and Adding Organic Matter	54
Adding Nitrogen	56
Soil Testing	60
Choosing Amendments	61
Organic Versus Synthetic Fertilizers	62

Chapter 8: Pruning Your Trees — 65

Why Do We Prune?	66
When to Prune	66
Tools	67
Approaches	67

Pruning Cuts	68
Pruning Young Trees	69
Pruning after the Third Year	72
Pruning Out Disease	73
Pruning an Established Tree	74
Pruning Hygiene	74
Pruning Peaches and Nectarines	74
Orchard Inspiration: Training Orchard Stewards at City Fruit, Seattle, WA	76

Chapter 9: Preventing Pests and Disease — 79

Boosting Biodiversity	80
Insect Deterrents	81
Monitoring your trees	82
Protective Sprays	83
A Few Common Diseases	88
A Few Common Pests	89
Orchard Inspiration: Piper's Orchard, Seattle, WA	90
The Holistic Approach	92

Part 4: The Harvest

Chapter 10: Anticipating the Harvest — 95

Orchard Inspiration: Not Far From The Tree, Toronto, ON	98

Part 5: Resources and Links

Resources and Links	101
Bibliography	107
Glossary	108
Acknowledgements	110

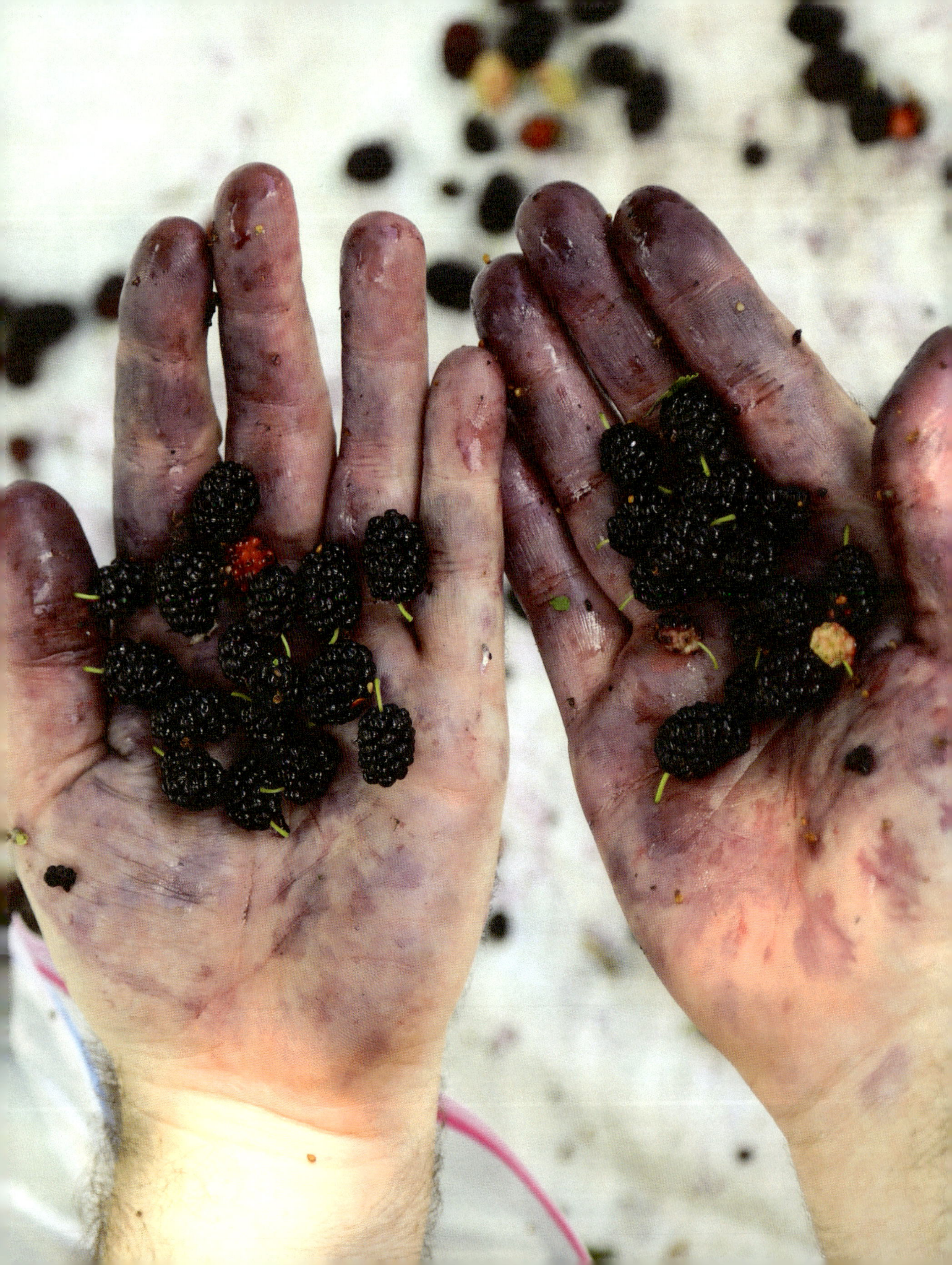

Chapter 1
Discovering Urban Orchards

I love healthy food. I love shopping for it, preparing it, and eating it. Buying fresh fruit and vegetables at local farmers' markets has been part of my life for many years. And yet for most of my life it never occurred to me to grow my own food. Up until 2006, I had never planted or cared for a garden. I was a writer, radio producer and filmmaker. I wasn't interested in gardening. I didn't see the magic in growing things at all.

Sometimes, when you see the world through someone else's eyes, it can change you. That's what happened to me. In 2005, I met my partner, Cliff Changoor, who grew up in Trinidad, where everyone he knew had gardens. When he and his father moved to Canada, they brought this tradition with them, growing tomatoes, peppers, peanuts, potatoes and much more.

We married in 2006, and that was the year Cliff decided that we should grow vegetables in our yard. I was hesitant. After all, wouldn't it be messy and a lot of work? Was it worth it when we can buy such great produce at our

From the moment our first nine fruit trees were planted in the park, we found ourselves on an incredible journey

local market? He kept bringing up the topic, and I kept resisting. Until finally, worn out from the ongoing conversation, I gave in.

"Ok fine. You can plant a garden – as long as you don't expect me to do any of the work. I'm not touching dirt," I said.

That summer, Cliff turned our backyard into a mini-farm and my skepticism turned to awe as I watched our garden grow into a place of incredible bounty. The tomatoes, beets, greens and herbs were so delicious. It amazed me that I could just go outside, harvest some lettuce, cucumbers and tomatoes, and have fresh salad on the table minutes later.

Soon, I started to work with Cliff in the garden. My brown thumb became greener. Like an enthusiastic new convert, I was hungry for knowledge. I enrolled in landscape design courses and in 2007, I worked with my neighbor Sherry Firing, a life-long gardener, to establish a gardening group in our community. We invited speakers to talk to us about native plants, xeriscaping and growing vegetables. The workshops were a hit, attracting up to 25 people each time.

The problem was that after the workshops, many in our group still didn't have the confidence to go out and get their hands dirty. I felt we needed a gardening project we could all work on together. In 2008, we heard about the establishment of community orchards in other cities in North America and the United Kingdom, and decided it would be fun for our group, called Growing for Green, to start a community orchard project in our local park. The volunteers would plant and care for the fruit trees together, to build community and to share the bounty.

Sherry and I proposed the idea to our city councilor, Joe Mihevc, and to Chris Martin of Toronto's Parks, Forestry and Recreation. With their support and the help of a volunteer, landscape architect Jane Hutton, we created a design for our orchard. Laura Reinsborough, of Toronto's popular fruit tree harvesting project Not Far From the Tree, helped us create a website and showed us how to apply for grants. In early 2009, we presented our orchard proposal at two community meetings. By June, we had permission to plant our first trees and the Ben Nobleman Park Community Orchard was born.

From the moment our first nine fruit trees were planted in the park, we found ourselves on an incredible journey. Like new parents with their first child, we had these trees but had no idea how to care for them. We made mistakes and reached for help. We brought in fruit-tree care experts from the Niagara region "Fruit Belt", a two-hour drive away, to teach us about winter and summer pruning, nutrition and how to protect our trees from pests and disease.

In 2010, we opened our workshops to the public, realizing that many others were in the same boat. Some wanted to plant fruit trees in their gardens but didn't know where to start. Others had planted young fruit trees that weren't thriving and they didn't know why. Yet others had older fruit trees on their properties that they didn't know how to care for.

We have learned so much over the years — mostly the hard way, by making mistakes. With this book, we hope to bring the lessons we learned out to the wider community. You may not have access to fruit tree care workshops in your community. Or you may find many of the fruit tree care books in the library are written for those who live in warmer climates where the growing conditions are very different.

This book is designed for people who live in the cooler regions of North America or Europe, where the summers are hot and the winter temperatures dip below zero. In these regions there is much that we have in common. At the same time, wherever people grow fruit, they will face their own unique problems.

While this book focuses on our experiences in Toronto, I include suggestions as to how other areas may differ and how to research solutions that will work in your part of the world.

For those of us who are willing to face the challenges of growing fruit in the city there are many rewards. Fruit trees beautify our neighbourhoods and bring our communities together. They clean our air and shade our gardens. And if we care for them well, they will give us one of the biggest gifts of all - the blessing of abundance of healthy organic fruit for decades to come.

Sherry, Cathy, Susan and Lynn at Ben Nobleman Park Community Orchard's Harvest Festival in 2010.

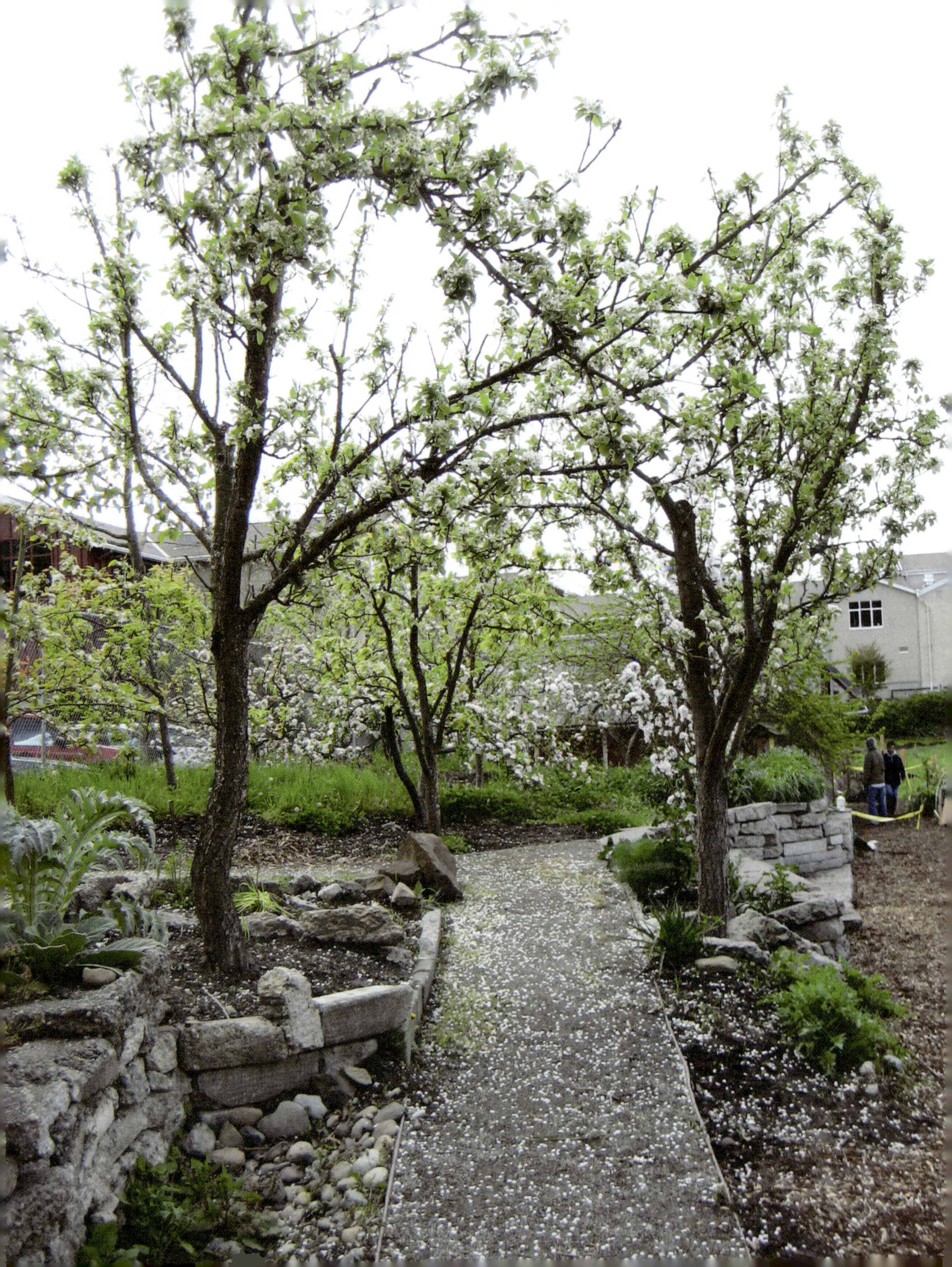

Chapter 2
Selecting Your Site

Where are you going to plant your orchard? Whether it is a community orchard, a school orchard or even if you are planting just one or two fruit trees in your yard, location is of the utmost importance. Here are some things to think about as you decide where to locate your trees.

Sun
Look for an area with full sun. Most fruit trees need 10 hours of sun a day during the growing season for maximum performance. Check your potential site a few times throughout the day, and throughout the growing season, to see how much sun it will have at different times of the day and year. Then choose the sunniest spot.

Irrigation
Make sure you have access to convenient irrigation. Do you have a hookup and hose that can reach your site? If not, you may need to fill buckets from a tap to water your trees two or three times a week while they are

getting established. If you are planting in a public space, ask the city to install an irrigation system; or raise money for that purpose.

Spacing

Look for an area where the trees roots will have room to grow. Avoid planting your trees too close to mature trees with extensive root systems that will curb the growth of your young tree or give it too much shade. If your tree is tucked too close to large shrubs, they will interfere with air circulation and could provide an ideal environment for fungal diseases to thrive.

Soil

Is the soil sandy? Or is it hard clay? Fruit trees generally like moist, well-drained and fertile soil that will hold moisture for a day or two. In most cases, general soil type can be amended with the annual addition of quality compost. But if there is construction waste, an old driveway or a poured concrete pad underneath your soil, your young tree won't stand much of a chance. Dig your hole before you buy your tree. It may save you from unpleasant surprises later on.

Drainage

Fruit trees don't like "wet feet" or standing water. Do not plant your trees in wet, swampy areas as this can cause root rot and other fatal diseases. This is the reason some orchardists like planting their trees on land that has a slight slope to it. It ensures that excess rainwater will drain away from their trees rather than sitting in puddles around the trees' roots.

Shelter

A bit of shelter is good for your tree and can protect it against a strong prevailing wind. A brick wall to the north of the tree could be helpful, as brick warms up in the sun and releases the heat at night, keeping your fruit trees warm and protecting them from a spring frost. A slope blocking prevailing winds may also protect your trees in harsh, windy weather.

Site Preparation

Once you have your site, you may want to wait a few months before buying your trees. That will give you time to do a soil test to amend your soil so that it will be more hospitable for fruit trees. (See Chapter 7.) And if you're not in a rush, you can weed and cultivate the soil where you will be planting your tree and sprinkle red clover, alfalfa or other green manure seeds, gently patting them down into the soil.

With regular watering, the soil should be covered with the green manure in less than three weeks, as long as you are seeding the soil during the growing season. At that point you can turn the soil, leaving the green manure in the ground. Let it decompose for about four weeks. As it does, it will increase the amount of organic matter and nutrients in your soil and that will help your trees thrive.

Ben Nobleman Park Orchard site map.

Central Locations

Instead of planting a fruit tree in a faraway corner of your garden that you never visit, plant it in a central location that you will walk by every day. Make note of any small changes in the tree. Are there spots on the leaves? Is there a clear oozy substance on one of the branches? Research the problem online to identify it and figure out how to treat it. Nip any problems in the bud so that diseases or insect infestations don't spread and debilitate your tree.

Grading

Planting on a steep slope may make it challenging to harvest and prune your trees. Imagine placing a ladder on this slope on a harvest day. If the slope is too steep, care and harvest may be dangerous.

Walkways and Driveways

While having a walkway or driveway lined with apple or apricot trees sounds like a great idea, it has to be done properly, with the trees a good distance away from the pathway or drive. Fruit trees drop fruit early in the season as the tree thins its crop naturally. Fruit will drop again nearer to harvest time. Nobody wants to slip on a half-squashed apple on a walkway … and nobody wants a juicy peach falling on her car – or on her head!

Alternative Locations

If your yard or local park doesn't look like it has the conditions needed for a healthy, happy orchard, you may consider other possible local planting locations. Orchards can be planted in churchyards, school grounds and near popular allotment gardens. Just make sure you have permission to plant and that the site is easily accessible for you and other volunteers.

Adopting Orchards

Instead of planting new fruit trees, you might consider adopting old ones. In the UK, many historic village orchards have been abandoned or left untended. Community groups have come in and adopted these orchards, renovated and maintained them, and now share the harvest. To read about a similar project in the United States, see the profile of Piper's Orchard in Chapter 9.

Orchard Inspiration: Walnut Way

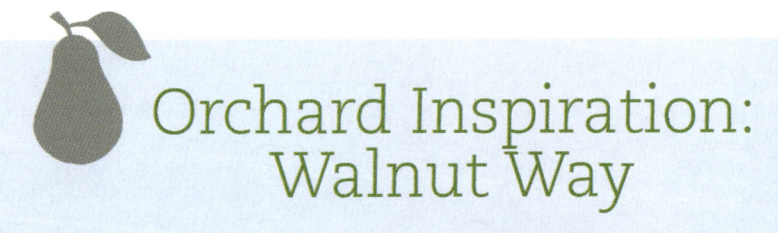

It's July 2013, and a once empty lot in the community of Walnut Way, Milwaukee, Wisconsin, is filled with peach trees. Their branches are heavy with fruit, which will be juicy and ripe for picking within a few weeks. These beautifully established fruit trees, planted almost a decade ago, hold enough peaches to feed residents, and the excess will be sold at a local farmer's market. But this is just one community garden amongst many in Walnut Way. Each garden is greener than the one before, bursting with organic edibles including cherries and pears, raspberries, blackberries, tomatoes, carrots and greens.

The abundance here is reminiscent of a community that once was. In the post-World War II period, Milwaukee emerged as an industrial powerhouse. In the 1940s, thousands of African Americans from the agricultural south came here in search of well paying jobs in the local brewing, railway and manufacturing industries. This was a time of segregation, and most of the black migrants settled in the neighbourhood surrounding Walnut Street. They worked hard and prospered. They bought homes and earned enough to pay for higher education for their children. Despite this new urban life, their agricultural heritage was never forgotten. Many planted and tended fruit trees and vegetable gardens on their properties, and they were highly self-sufficient.

In the 1970s, the American Dream in Walnut Way turned into a nightmare as the result of globalization. Between 1967 and 2001, the city lost 69 percent of its manufacturing jobs and the black community was hit hard. Companies closed down and the residents of Walnut Way lost their main sources of income. To add insult to injury, a highway was built through the neighbourhood, destroying homes, tearing apart the business district and slicing the community in two. Property values plummeted and unemployment was endemic. A sense of hopelessness grew as crime rates and social problems soared.

"We planted the fruit trees to give the community a feeling of abundance rather than scarcity," says Larry Adams. He and his wife Sharon are amongst the founders of the Walnut Way Conservation Corporation, which was established in 1998. Since then, the group has worked to rebuild the neighbourhood, drive out crime, and restore century-old homes. The fruit trees and gardens have grown alongside other initiatives including community-building events, artistic projects and job training for young people. Today Walnut Way is a model for other disadvantaged neighbourhoods across North America - and one of the very first steps was to plant peach trees in an empty lot.

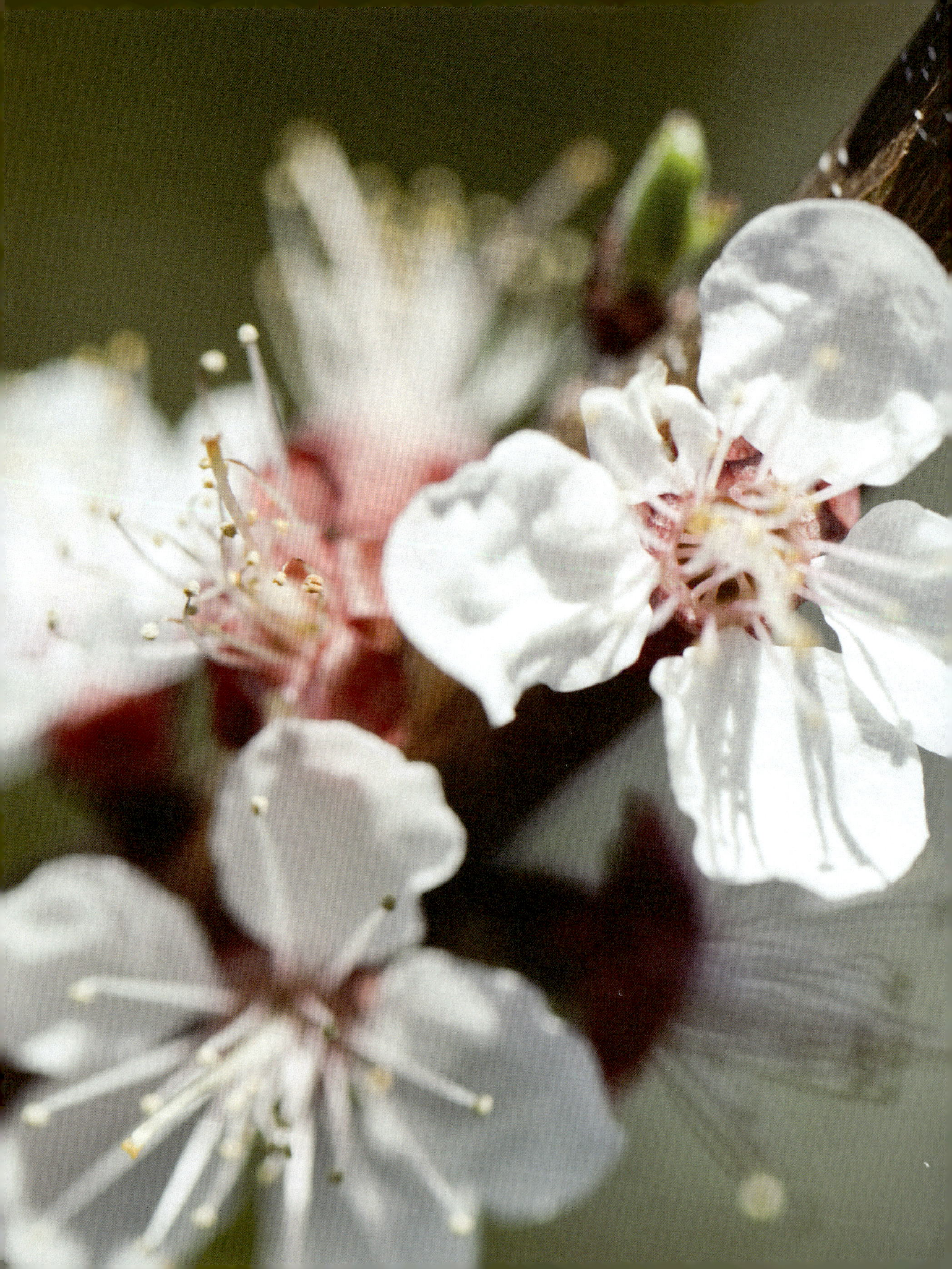

Chapter 3
Parts of a Fruit Tree

As we were making a plan for our orchard, I went to the library and found plenty of books about growing fruit trees. I was interested in landscape design tips. I loved the photos and descriptions of mouth-watering fruit cultivars. And yet, if any of those books had a chapter on tree biology, I would skip that part. After all, our goal was to grow trees so that we could eat and share the fruit. Why get bogged down with the scientific details?

That was one of my first mistakes. Everything we do to care for a tree relates to some aspect of its biology. When you understand how your tree grows, caring for it becomes more intuitive.

Blossoms and Fruit

In the early spring of 2012, after an unseasonably warm winter, the three apricot trees in Ben Nobleman Park Community Orchard came into bloom weeks early. The trees looked great after a long, bleak winter, and we were optimistic about our harvest that year. Early blossoms should result in an earlier harvest, right?

Blossoms and the Aspiring Orchardist

- **Learn to keep an eye** on your blossoms in the early spring. If there is a frost, you will know the blossoms have survived if the stigma has not turned black.

- **Honeybees hibernate** when the weather is cold (below 10 degrees Celsius or 50 degrees Fahrenheit). Fluctuating weather in the spring can result in low pollination rates. For instance, your trees may blossom early as a result of a warm spell, but if the weather then becomes cooler, it may be too cold for the bees to pollinate your trees.

- **Mason bees can also pollinate** fruit trees and they can tolerate lower temperatures. Install a mason bee "condo" to attract them to your garden.

- **Not all fruit trees** are pollinated by bees. The pawpaw tree is a native tree in parts of North America that is pollinated instead by carrion flies and beetles. And instead of having sweet smelling blossoms, the pawpaw blossoms smell a bit like rotten meat!

- **One of the most** important things you do when you select your fruit tree is to ensure that it will pollinate successfully by either buying a self-pollinating tree or ensuring your tree has a pollination partner. (See chapter 4) since a fruit tree that does not successfully pollinate will not produce fruit.

- **It takes a lot of the tree's energy** to produce blossoms. So we add nutrition to the soil before bloom time in order to ensure the tree has enough energy to blossom and fruit properly. (See Chapter 7)

"Not necessarily," said Ken Slingerland, retired soft fruit expert from the Ontario Ministry of Food and Rural Affairs, during a visit to the orchard. It was mid-March and the risk of a spring frost had not passed. Ken warned us that there was a good chance that our blossoms would die if the temperatures dipped well below freezing — and dead blossoms mean no fruit.

Each day, I checked the evening forecast, and temperatures were expected to dip anywhere from minus 3 to minus 7 degrees Celsius (26 to 19 degrees Fahrenheit). In the morning, I'd scramble up to the orchard to inspect the blossoms. If the stigmas (part of the female reproductive structure of the flower) were still yellow, the blossoms had survived. If they were black, the blossoms had died and my dreams of a great apricot harvest that year would be dashed.

So it's helpful to understand the form and function of fruit-tree blossoms. Think of blossoms as beautiful packages that hold and protect the sexual organs that allow trees to reproduce. This is how it works:

1. Bloom Time

In the spring, fruit trees blossom. While we humans come out to admire the flowers after a long winter, pollinators such as bees and other flying insects also flock to the trees. In the case of bees, their goal is to gather nectar from the blossoms to bring back to their hives. Over time, the nectar will evaporate, thicken and become honey.

2. Pollination

While collecting the nectar, these bees bumble around, getting messy as they negotiate their way around the flowers. Pollen from the anthers, or male organs of the flowers, sticks to their bodies. When the bees fly off to gather nectar on neighboring trees, the pollen will rub off and onto the stigma (or female organ) of the new flower they are visiting.

3. Fertilization

Next the pollen germinates – or begins to sprout – and grows down the style into the ovule, where the male and female genetic materials unite, producing what will one day be a fruit's seed. In order to protect the seed, a fleshy area grows around it. This fleshy material will become the part of the fruit that humans and wildlife eat.

4. Proliferation

When the fruit is ripe, we pick it off the tree, eat it and discard the pit. Or an animal or bird may eat the fruit and excrete the seed. Either way, that seed or pit, once embedded in the soil, has the potential to grow into a new tree. That tree may have some of the characteristics of each of its parent trees. Nevertheless, the new tree will be genetically unique and produce a unique variety of fruit.

So how similar will fruit grown from a random seed be to that of the parent tree? Apples have extreme diversity in their DNA. Even if both parent trees produce sweet, tasty fruit, the seedling tree may well produce apples that are hard and sour. Bananas, on the other hand, are less genetically diverse, and the fruit is more likely to taste similar to the parents' fruit.

Anatomy of an apple blossom

Buds and Leaves

Leaves tell us so much about the health of our trees. Do they have strange orange spots on them? This might be rust. Are your tree leaves turning a dull yellow in the middle of the summer? This might signify a nutritional deficiency. This is how leaves function:

1. Winter Dormancy

In the winter, trees are bare after losing their leaves in the fall. Where the leaves once were you can find small buds along the branches. Each bud is a tough, protective sheath that holds inside it everything the tree needs to produce a new leaf or a blossom. The buds can withstand frost and harsh winds, protecting their precious contents until spring.

2. Spring Swelling

In early spring, the days become longer, temperatures rise and the buds on our fruit trees swell. Tender young leaves or delicate blossoms are growing inside them. Soon, the buds will pop open, exposing a bit of green inside, evidence of the new leaf or blossom. Soon the hard scales of the buds will fall away. The blossoms will open up and the leaves will slowly unfurl.

3. Gathering Sunshine

New leaves then have to produce food for their trees. What is important to us is how they do this. A healthy leaf contains a green pigment called chlorophyll that absorbs light energy from the sun. The underside of the leaf has holes or pores (called stomata) that absorb carbon dioxide from the air. The leaves convert those ingredients into food to nourish the tree. The byproducts are water and oxygen, which are released back into the air through the stomata.

Leaf and Fruit Buds

FLOWER BUD
LEAF BUD
FRUITING SPUR

Buds of an apple tree: Leaf buds are flatter and fruit buds more rounded. Fruit buds sometimes grow in groupings called "spurs".

4. Autumn

As the days get shorter and the weather cools, trees prepare for dormancy. By this time the tree has stored enough food (glucose) in its branches, trunk and roots to last it through the winter. Soon, as the chlorophyll disappears from the leaves and the leaves change colours and fall off, and the cycle will begin again the following spring.

Leaves and the Aspiring Orchardist

- **Leaves are incredibly efficient** at taking in external nutrients, so many orchardists brush their trees' leaves with compost tea or use foliar sprays, like diluted liquid fish emulsion or diluted seaweed extract, to give their trees a nutritional boost.

- **When spraying** your tree's leaves with foliar sprays or with organic fungicides like sulphur (see Chapter 9) make sure you spray the underside of the leaf, as the stomata absorb inputs more quickly and efficiently than the upper side of the leaf.

- **The stomata usually open** in the morning and close at night. They may also close during the day as a result of extreme heat or harsh weather conditions, so the best time to spray your trees is in the early morning.

- **When there is a drought**, the leaves of fruit trees continue releasing water from the stomata, so your leaves will look droopy and dehydrated. That's a sign that it's time to water as soon as possible.

- **Disease or insect** infestations can debilitate or kill your tree by attacking the leaves. Eaten or diseased leaves photosynthesize poorly, making it impossible for leaves to produce food. Growths on the stomata can prevent the absorption of carbon dioxide and the release of water.

Soon, the buds will pop open and you'll be able to see a bit of green inside, evidence of the new leaf or blossom

Roots

Tree roots anchor the tree into the ground but they have another essential role. They extract water and nutrients from the soil, which are then transported around the tree. This is how it works:

1. Planting

You plant your tree. If you are planting a young, bare root tree in the spring, you can see its thick woody roots. Once planted, they will stretch out far beyond the edge of the tree's canopy, to reach up to four times the tree's diameter. Usually tree roots live in the top 6 to 24 inches of the soil.

2. Feeder Roots

Soon, feeder roots, often with a diameter of less than 1.6 cm (1/16th of an inch), begin emerging from the woody roots. They grow outward and upward from the woody roots in order to absorb minerals, water and oxygen from the upper surface of the soil. Together with the woody roots, feeder roots anchor the tree to the ground and stabilize the soil. But while woody roots are permanent, feeder roots are temporary, and die each year in the late fall. New feeder roots will grow the following spring.

Tree Roots

Tree roots extend as far as the tree's canopy and beyond.

3. Root Hairs

Feeder roots are covered with tiny root hairs, which you can only see with the help of a powerful microscope. Without those root hairs, the feeder roots would not be able to do their job and collect the minerals the tree needs from the soil. The root hairs are capable of taking inorganic nutrients like calcium, boron, potassium, magnesium and more into the tree. In order to function properly, however, the root hairs need moisture. So if your tree doesn't have enough water, it will not only be dehydrated, it will also become nutritionally impoverished.

4. Expansion

Roots grow towards areas in the soil where water, oxygen and minerals are available. If the soil is highly compacted, the roots cannot push through. Similarly, if you put something heavy on top of the soil near a healthy tree (anything from a large can of paint to a parked car), the soil will be compacted, feeder roots will be crushed and new feeder roots will have no room to grow. The result? The tree can't get access to the oxygen, water and minerals it needs to survive. This can seriously compromise the health of your tree.

Root Growth and the Aspiring Orchardist

- **If you park a car** on a tree's roots, or even put a heavy object on them, the root hairs will be compressed or damaged and that results in the tree being more susceptible to fungal root diseases. Signs of this in the upper portion of the tree include yellowing foliage, reduced growth and branch dieback. These are also signs of mineral deficiencies – which makes sense since dead root hairs can't collect minerals from the soil.

- **If you plant** your young tree too close to an older tree, the roots of the two trees will compete for water, minerals and oxygen. The larger and more established tree will most likely win out and your young tree may be nutrient-deprived.

- **Too much mulch** can prevent water and oxygen from reaching the roots. When mulching the trees, place just five to eight cm (two or three inches) of compressed mulch in a donut shape around the tree, keeping the mulch 12 cm (five inches away) from the trunk.

- **Roots are thicker and woodier** near the trunk of a mature tree. Thinner feeder roots are under the canopy of the tree and closer to its dripline. If nutrients are added on the area near the trunk, they will not be absorbed. Focus nutrient applications (including compost and well-rotted manure) to the area above the feeder roots.

- **Roots need to be hydrated** in order to perform their function of drawing minerals into the tree, so a dehydrated tree will also become malnourished. Your tree needs to be well watered. But at the same time, overwatering can cause problems. Fruit trees don't like "wet feet," so if they are in soggy soil, the excess standing water can cause root rot and fungal diseases. It's a fine balance.

- **Young fruit trees** have a limited root system and cannot compete for food and water with other plants, especially nutrient-hogging weeds like dandelions, vetch, alfalfa or thistle. If you allow your tree to be crowded out by weeds, it will become dehydrated and malnourished. Ensure that there are absolutely no competing plants within one meter (or 3.3 feet) around the base of your tree. Weeding is an important part of fruit tree care.

Trunk and Bark

We know that tree trunks give structure and shape to the tree. But they do so much more than that. The tree trunk is home to the tree's cambium layer which transports minerals, nutrients and water from the roots into the rest of the tree. The cambium layer is made up of the phloem, cambium and xylem and each sub layer has a different function.

1. Bark

Bark is the thick, protective outer sheath of a tree trunk. It is perforated with millions of tiny pores called lenticels, which allow carbon dioxide from the air to pass through to the layers of living cells underneath the bark. On most trees, it's hard to see the lenticels with the bare eye. On cherry trees, they are easier to spot and look like dark horizontal lines all over the tree trunk.

2. Phloem

There are three layers of living cells underneath the bark. The first layer, called the phloem, is soft and spongy and acts as a nutritional superhighway. After the leaves produce glucose, the phloem transports this sugary substance to other parts of the tree giving it energy to grow and produce fruit.

3. Cambium

The second layer is the cambium, a thin tissue where tree growth takes place. Cambium cells are constantly dividing, producing food-transporting phloem cells closer to the bark of the tree and xylem, or wood cells, towards the core of the tree.

4. Xylem

The xylem, which is the third layer, is made up of two parts. Closest to the cambium is the sapwood, living cells that transport water and minerals from the roots up to the leaves. The xylem also produces a layer of dead cells called the heartwood, which becomes part of the dense core of the tree.

5. Thickening Trunk

As the cambium divides, the tree trunk gets thicker, with more and more heartwood being produced. The xylem and the phloem will always remain just under the outer bark, circulating food, water and minerals around the tree. Each year, as this process continues, the trunk will get stronger, sturdier and thicker.

Tree Layers

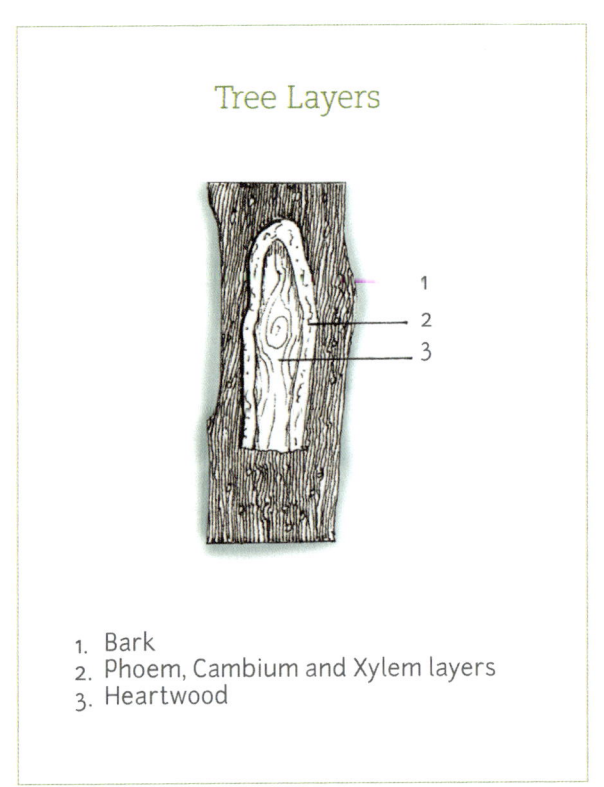

1. Bark
2. Phoem, Cambium and Xylem layers
3. Heartwood

Trunk & Bark and the Aspiring Orchardist

• **Water your tree's roots**, not its bark. Sprinklers spray water on your tree's trunk and waterborne diseases can then move into the tree via a wound in the bark. Instead, water trees roots by hand or use a drip hose.

• **Certain types of insects** can bore into the wood of the bark – especially if there is a wound in the tree – and lay eggs inside. Some may carry fungal diseases, which can grow under the bark and prevent the phloem and xylem from transporting nutrients, water and minerals, weakening and even killing the tree.

• **The lenticels on the bark can get clogged** up with dirt when the tree is located on a busy, polluted road. This will make it hard for the tree to absorb carbon dioxide and release oxygen, and can stress the tree.

• **Tree trunks can be damaged** by extreme frosts or they can even get sunburn. One way to protect them is to paint the trunks with diluted white paint right up to the lower branches of the tree, which reflects light away from the trunk and protects it (see Chapter 9).

• **Mulching annually** is great. Adding quality compost around the tree is great. But pushing the mulch and or compost right up to your tree's trunk can trap moisture and cause the trunk to rot.

Fruit trees are made up of two different trees that have been grafted, or fused together, to function as a single tree

The Grafted Tree

Up until now we've discussed how trees function, and that information will help us to care for our fruit trees. But fruit trees are often a little different from trees you find in nature. That's because most fruit trees are made up of two different trees that have been grafted, or fused together, to function as a single tree.

One tree provides the "rootstock," which will contribute a root system and a small amount of trunk to the newly grafted tree. The rootstock will be the type of tree that has great qualities that you might want your fruit tree to have, like hardiness, disease resistance, vigorous growth patterns, an early flowering time or a compact size.

The second tree provides the fruiting branches. It is called the fruitwood, or scion, and it's actually a branch clipped from a tree with tasty fruit that you'd like to reproduce. These two trees will be fused together through grafting, so that the fruitwood branch will become the trunk of the tree and its buds will produce branches that reach out from the trunk.

When grafting is done properly, the cambium layer of the two components match up and grow together, allowing the tree to function as a single unit. Usually, you can see where the two trees were grafted, as there is a bulge at the base of the trunk of the tree. Above the bulge (or graft union) is the fruitwood. Below the bulge is the rootstock.

Grafted Trees and the Aspiring Orchardist

- **Fruit trees have been grafted** for thousands of years and records of grafted trees go back as far as ancient Rome.

- **Grafting is common** because it can take five to 12 years until a tree grown from seed is ready to produce fruit - and even then, the chances of the "seedling" tree producing tasty fruit is minimal, due to genetic diversity. (see "Proliferation" on page 15).

- **In order for grafting to be successful,** the root stock and the scion need to be compatible. For example, apple scions should be grafted onto apple root stock and pear scions should be grafted onto pear root stock.

- **Varieties of grafted trees** are often called cultivars (or cultivated varieties) which means that human intervention is necessary to clone the tree and propagate the variety.

- **When planting your tree,** make sure that the graft union (the bulge where the root stock has been fused onto the scion) is about 5 cm (2 inches) above the soil line. If you bury the graft union, the scion may grow roots and then your tree will not benefit from the positive traits of the rootstock.

Understanding Grafting: The Story of the McIntosh Apple

The story of the McIntosh apple helps illustrate why we graft fruit trees and how this process of cultivating varieties has resulted in the spread of popular varieties around the world.

In late 1811, John McIntosh was clearing land to build a house in Southeastern Ontario when he discovered a very special apple tree. This self-seeded tree produced the most delicious apples that he had ever tasted. They were crisp, firm, sweet and juicy.

Friends and family were impressed, so John extracted seeds from the fruit and grew seedlings to give away or sell to others. But the fruit those seedlings produced never tasted or looked like the fruit of his original tree.

Almost 25 years later, an itinerant farmhand showed John's son Allen how to clone the tree by grafting its branches onto seedling trees. These new trees produced fruit that looked and tasted exactly like the parent tree. The grafted trees were a hit, and selling them became a successful business for the family.

Allen grafted more and more trees and sold them all over eastern Ontario. He named the variety "McIntosh Red." Soon the name was shortened to McIntosh and this apple is now one of the most popular apple varieties in the world.

Today there are millions of McIntosh trees around the world. Like all cloned or grafted varieties, all are made from a cutting from the original tree or one of its descendants.

The McIntosh apple is a result of grafting techniques.

GROWING URBAN ORCHARDS

Atago Asian Pear
Grafted Apr 2010

Chapter 4
Selecting Your Fruit Trees

One of the first lessons that we learned in planting the Ben Nobleman Park Community Orchard is why you should not leave it to the last minute to order your fruit trees. It was June, 2009, by the time we received permission to plant fruit trees in our park. Since fruit trees are best planted in the early spring, this was late in the season and the stock at most of our local garden centres was already picked over.

During the winter, we had spent hours in the library researching cultivars that would work well in our orchard park. Little did we know that few of these cultivars are available for sale in our region. Even if we were lucky and our local garden centres had stocked some of our chosen varieties, by June they were sold out. The few trees that remained were often left behind for a reason. They might have had damaged buds or broken branches, or their shape wasn't ideal for supporting fruit.

Selecting the right trees for your conditions will go a long way to ensuring your orchard's success. With the right trees, you'll enjoy a generous harvest and you will face fewer challenges in managing pests and disease. With the wrong ones, you may find yourself pouring your love and energy into a sickly tree that never produces fruit. Some of our choices were good. Some were not. In this chapter, we will take you through the steps of choosing a fruit tree that will thrive in your yard or park.

Hardiness

What gardening zone are you in? Look at a plant hardiness zone map online to find out. Tree labels will have a zone hardiness indicator so that you can choose a tree that will thrive in your conditions. If you live in the Arctic region, your plant hardiness zone will be zero, meaning that few plants can thrive in your climate. In Canada, for example, Edmonton, Alberta, is in zone 3 and Regina, Saskatchewan, is in zone 2. Toronto, Ontario, is in zone 5 or 6 depending on where you live in the city. The rule of thumb is that you can plant a tree that is hardy to your zone and up to three zones colder.

Examples of Fruit Tree Zones and Varieties

So lets say that you want to plant fruit trees in a zone 4 garden. Which ones might you choose? Have a look at the chart below.

Another way to think about hardiness is to look at how cold your climate gets and to see if the buds of your fruit tree (from which flowers and then fruit will form) will survive the coldest weather in your region. In general, peach and nectarine flower or fruit buds will begin to die at minus 20 degrees Celsius (minus 4 Fahrenheit). Plums and apricots flower or fruit buds will begin to die at minus 23 degrees Celsius (minus 9.4 Fahrenheit). Apples, cherries and pears are the hardiest of the bunch, as their flower or fruit buds can survive up to minus 25 degrees Celsius (minus 13 Fahrenheit) and below depending on the individual cultivar.

Disease Resistance

As much as we love supermarket fruit like Royal Gala apples and Bartlett pears, these types of fruit trees may not be the best ones to grow at home. Many are cultivars that were designed for large-scale growing, and often they need to be sprayed regularly with chemical pesticides and fungicides that most home growers would avoid. If you are growing your trees organically, opt for disease-resistant cultivars such as Liberty, Freedom or Prima apples. Find a nursery near you that specializes in disease-resistant trees and ask them what varieties they recommend.

VARIETY	HARDINESS	WOULD IT WORK IN A ZONE 4 GARDEN?
Sweetheart Sweet Cherries	Hardy to zone 5	No. This tree requires a warmer climate.
Rescue Crab Apples	Hardy to zone 2	Sure. This tree would even survive in zones 2, 3, 4 and 5.
Red Gravenstein Apple	Hardy to zone 4	Yes. This tree would be happy in a zone 4 garden.

When looking at varieties, ensure that any tree that needs cross-pollination is planted near a pollination partner.

Tree Size

All fruit trees are grown on rootstock that will determine the size of the mature tree. If you have a small garden, you may choose a dwarf tree that will grow no higher than 1.8 metres (six feet) tall and will be easy to harvest. If you have a larger garden and want more fruit, you will probably opt for a more rugged semi-dwarf tree that will grow up to 4.6 metres (15 feet) tall. Full-sized trees can grow to up to 12 metres (40 feet) tall. Unless you want to harvest or prune your tree by leaning out of your second-floor window (this is not recommended), it might be best to avoid a tree this large.

The serviceberry is an easy-to-grow native tree that has wonderful fruit.

Cross-Pollinating Trees

Some trees are self-pollinating. So if you buy one tree, it can pollinate itself and those pollinated blossoms will then set fruit (see Chapter 3). Other trees are cross-pollinating (also known as "self-sterile"). So if you buy just one of those trees without planting an appropriate partner tree nearby, you will be fruitless forever. When looking at varieties, ensure that any tree that needs cross-pollination is planted near a pollination partner. Good nurseries will have a pollination chart to help you, but on page 29 I've outlined a few general rules."

Self-Pollinating Fruit Trees

When you have limited space, self-pollinating trees are a great choice as they will produce fruit even if they are planted on their own.

Here are a few examples of self-pollinating fruit trees. They are also known as "self-fertile":

Goldcot Apricot
(Hardy to Zone 4)

Veecot Apricot
(Hardy to Zone 5)

Stella Sweet Cherry
(Hardy to Zone 5)

Lapins Sweet Cherry
(Hardy to Zone 5)

Montmorency Sour Cherry
(Hardy to Zone 4)

Reliance Peach
(Hardy to Zone 5)

Greengage Plum
(Hardy to Zone 4)

Stanley Plum
(Hardy to Zone 5)

Toka Plum
(Hardy to Zone 4)

Self-polinating trees are a good choice if you have a small garden.

Staggering the Harvest

If you have space for more than one tree in your orchard, ensure that your fruit will ripen at different times in the season by looking up the estimated harvest dates for each of your trees. Perhaps you'll want to include cherries that are ripe in July, plums that ripen in August and apples that are ready to harvest in September. By staggering your harvest, you can have fresh fruit throughout the season, and you avoid the syndrome some call "fruit fatigue" – when you have so much of a single type of fruit that you don't know what to do with it all. If, on the other hand, you are planting a school orchard, a fruitless summer followed by a generous harvest in September and October might be just what you are looking for, as the students are back in school and there will be enough fruit to share around.

Some fruit trees produce fruit that is best for cooking, baking or canning

Eating, Cooking or Canning

Some fruit is great for eating straight off the tree. Other types are best for cooking or canning. Yet others are best for making cider, juice or fruit wine. What types of fruit do you want to grow? As you research cultivars, read the descriptions to make sure you're growing fruit that you will enjoy. Consider including one cultivar that is good for storage, so you'll be able to enjoy fresh fruit well into the winter months.

Heirloom Trees

For thousands of years, people have grown fruit trees organically. The fruit may not have been perfect looking; sometimes it was wormy or scabby. Often the fruit was tart, unlike the modern varieties we eat today, which were

General Rules for Cross-Polinating Tree Varieties

Often trees need a partner that is not identical to them. So a McIntosh apple will not cross-pollinate with another McIntosh apple, and a Bartlett pear will not cross-pollinate with a Bartlett pear. Here are a few more pollination rules.

- **Trees cross-pollinate** within their fruit group. So pears cross-pollinate with pears. Sweet cherries cross-pollinate with sweet cherries. Apples cross-pollinate with other apples, and so forth.

- **Trees need to flower** at the same time in order to cross-pollinate. So an early flowering cherry tree will not cross-pollinate with a cherry tree that flowers later in the season. Check a pollination chart to ensure compatibility. These charts are available from specialist fruit tree nurseries or online.

- **Most sour cherry, apricot and peach** trees are self-pollinating, so they can be planted on their own and will successfully produce fruit.

- **Most apple, pear, sweet cherry and plum** trees are not self-pollinating, so they need to be planted alongside a compatible tree if you want a harvest.

- **European plums** (Prunus domestica) and Japanese plums (Prunus salicina) do not cross-pollinate because they blosson at different times.

- **Crabapples are wonderful pollinators** for many varieties of apple trees because they are consistent bloomers and have large amounts of viable pollen.

- **Sour cherry trees and sweet cherry trees** will not pollinate each other.

- **Asian pears cross-pollinate** with other Asian pears or with European pears.

- **Some types of fruit trees,** like Jonagold apple trees, have sterile pollen. These so-called "triploid" trees can be pollinated by another apple tree, but the triploid cannot return the favour. If you plant a triploid tree, plant it with two other compatible trees that will pollinate each other as well as the triploid.

- **Some trees, like Lodi, Liberty or Gala** apples, are able to pollinate themselves, but they'll set more fruit if they are pollinated by another compatible cultivar.

- **Some fruit trees have been grafted** so you can have four or five types of apples on one tree. These multi-graft trees can be planted alone because the blossoms from one cultivar will pollinate the blossoms from another.

- **Multi-graft trees,** however, are usually not made up of disease-resistant cultivars and so they may not always be the best choice.

- **While bees will travel 2-3 km** (1.2-1.9 miles) to seek the nectar from fruit trees, there is a greater success with cross-pollination if the trees are planted close together.

Orchard Inspiration: City of Calgary Community Orchard Research Project

In 2009, when the City of Calgary launched their Community Orchard Research Project, they knew they had homework to do. Over the years, many community gardens had sprouted up around the city, and gardeners were interested in planting fruit trees in their local parks as well. But it is not easy to grow fruit trees in Calgary due to the city's unique weather conditions.

The problem is not Calgary's zone 3 climate. There are many fruit tree varieties that can withstand cold, zone 3 winters. It's the periodic chinooks, or warm winds that blow in during the winter, that make it hard to grow fruit. Due to Calgary's geographic location, these winds can bring in a week or more of summer temperatures in the heart of the winter, and that can trigger leaf and fruit buds to open early. Open buds will die when the more seasonal freezing weather returns. If fruit buds die in the winter, they take with them any hope for a harvest that year.

"When we launched the community orchard program, everyone wanted an orchard in their park. We don't want to set communities up for failure, so it was important to help them choose the right trees," says Jill-Anne Spence, Urban Forestry Lead for the City of Calgary, who explains that their solution was to work with researchers at the University of Saskatchewan Fruit Program, whose expertise is in selecting and breeding cold-hardy fruiting plants.

The experts identified a number of fruit trees that might survive Calgary's climate, including: Honey Crisp, Rescue and Parkland apples (all hardy to zone 3), Rescue Crabapples (hardy to zone 2), Golden Spice and Early Gold pear (hardy to zone 3) and Valentine, Cupid and Romeo cherries (hardy to Zone 2a) as well as a number of varieties of apricot trees, gooseberries, honeyberries (also called hascaps) and strawberries. In 2009, these fruiting trees and shrubs were planted at four pilot sites.

So far, so good. Follow-up studies show that most of the trees are doing well. The apples, apricots and cherries have a high survival rate. The pears, on the other hand, were not as successful. If the city decides to expand the program, they will know which varieties to recommend, and that will give community groups a head start when they plant their new orchards.

"We want our programs to be successful, especially when you are harnessing volunteer energy to care for the trees. We wanted to make sure the trees we were recommending would have a better chance for success," Spence says.

developed to satisfy our society's sweet tooth. But some of these age-old varieties are great for pies and sauce, and some may be naturally resistant to disease. The best way to find out which heirloom trees will thrive in your area is to speak to someone who tends a local historic orchard (often linked to local history museums and historic sites).

Native Trees

There are other fruit trees that we overlook when planning an orchard. In much of North America, serviceberries (*Amelanchier*) are a native tree or shrub with small, berry-like fruit about the size of a blueberry. The fruit, which starts off red and turns purple-black when ripe, is sweet and delicious on cereal, in muffins or in pies. They are easy to grow (no cross-pollination necessary) and if you don't eat the fruit, that's okay because the birds will. The American elderberry (*Sambucus canadensis*) is a beautiful woody native shrub. Its berries can be made into preserves and its blossoms can be battered and fried or used to make tea or elderflower "champagne." However, education is important around the American elderberry, as the leaves are poisonous and the raw fruit can cause stomach upsets.

In Southern Ontario, we can also plant pawpaws (*Asimina*), a native North American tree with dramatic, tropical-looking leaves that produces a fruit that some say tastes a bit like banana. Pawpaw fruit is easily bruised, so it's not marketed in the shops. It's an understory tree, so it enjoys a bit of shade but it will grow well in full sun, too. You do need to plant two or more trees to ensure pollination. If you live outside Ontario, talk to the staff at your local garden centre. Can they suggest any native trees with edible fruit that are good to grow in your region?

Nut Trees

When we first started to develop the idea for our community orchard, we were excited about adding nut trees to our orchard. Hazelnuts grow very well in our climate and they are a beautiful plant, too. But after a bit of research, I realized that might be a waste of our time. In Toronto's urban environment, there are few natural predators to keep the squirrel population down. So we have a huge population of squirrels who will demolish any nut crop we grow before we humans ever enjoy the harvest. In the end, we planted two shagbark hickory trees just for fun and not for harvest. If the squirrels want hazelnuts or other tasty nuts, let them plant their own trees.

On the other hand, many of the other community and school orchards that I have worked with across Canada live in more rural environments, where squirrels are not a problem. Nut trees that they might consider include pecans, which are beautiful native shade trees. Hazelnuts are a great option. A walnut tree may also be a good choice, but beware! Walnut trees secrete chemicals into the soil that prevent other plants from growing nearby, so do not plant your new walnut tree anywhere near a flower or vegetable garden. Find a local nut nursery to discuss your options.

Ordering Trees in the Fall for Spring Planting

Once you've done your research and know which trees you want, it's time to order your trees. Specialist fruit tree nurseries often sell out long before prime planting season in the spring. So it's best to order your trees in the fall, the year before you are planting to ensure you get what you want. That also gives you the time to improve your soil by planting green manure (see Chapter 2) as a way of preparing it for your young trees.

Bare Root Versus Potted Trees

Potted trees are an easy option. While you can only plant bare root trees in the early spring, you can plant a potted tree almost any time during the gardening season. Bare root trees are often younger and smaller (they will be sent to you in the post) but they adapt to their new conditions better and grow much more quickly than their once-potted colleagues. With bare root trees you will find you have a wider selection of trees to choose from, including hard-to-source disease-resistant cultivars or heirloom varieties. When your bare root tree arrives, you need to plant it as soon as possible because it can't survive long without the nutrition and protection that soil provides. But planting a bare root tree is not difficult and you'll find how-to instructions in Chapter 5 of this book.

Inspecting Your New Tree

If you are choosing a tree from your local garden centre, look at it carefully. Does it have a straight trunk? Choose a tree with a balanced structure, that has an upright central leader and branches that stretch out in four directions (read Chapter 8 for information on structure). Make sure the buds look healthy, as damaged buds mean fewer options later when you are pruning. And make sure the tree looks healthy. If there are orange blotches on the leaves, if the leaves are turning yellow, or if dark ooze is coming off any of the branches, you should choose another specimen.

Orchardist Norm Herbert with a bare root fruit tree.

Transport Trees Carefully

Once you've found your perfect tree, take it home carefully! Damage can happen on the trip home from the nursery if the tree is stuffed into the car and buds are scratched and destroyed. Remember, those buds are the future architecture of your tree, as each has the potential to grow into a strong, fruit-bearing branch. Treat them with care.

Types of Fruit

When you think about fruit that you can grow in a cool climate, you think of apples, pears, cherries and plums. But there are many other types of fruit that you may not have heard of that you can grow successfully in an urban environment. These are available at specialist nurseries:

Asian Pear Trees are disease-resistant trees that have great fall colours. They produce sweet and crunchy fruit that looks more like an apple.

Chum Shrubs are hardy, easy-care shrubs that produce a cherry-plum hybrid. The fruit looks like a cherry but is slightly larger. Chums can be eaten fresh or baked into pies.

Plumcot or Pluot Shrubs and Trees produce a plum-apricot hybrid fruit that looks like an apricot but has plum-like flesh. Some varieties are hardy and disease-resistant.

European Plum Trees produce fruit that is often best dried into prunes or preserved as jams.

Japanese Plum Trees produce fruit that is terrific eaten fresh off the tree, but can also be canned, dried or turned into preserves.

American Plum Shrubs are resistant to disease. The native varieties are best for cooking or canning, but some varieties that have been crossed with Japanese plums are delicious eaten fresh, too.

Crabapple Trees are beautiful trees with prolific blossoms, and while the fruit may be a bit tart to eat raw, they make fantastic crabapple jelly

Mulberry Trees are disease and pest-resistant and have sweet berries that are great eaten fresh or used to make jam.

Quince Trees can be attractive trees with lovely blossoms, and the pear-shaped fruit, which is too hard to eat raw, is usually used to make jam or jelly.

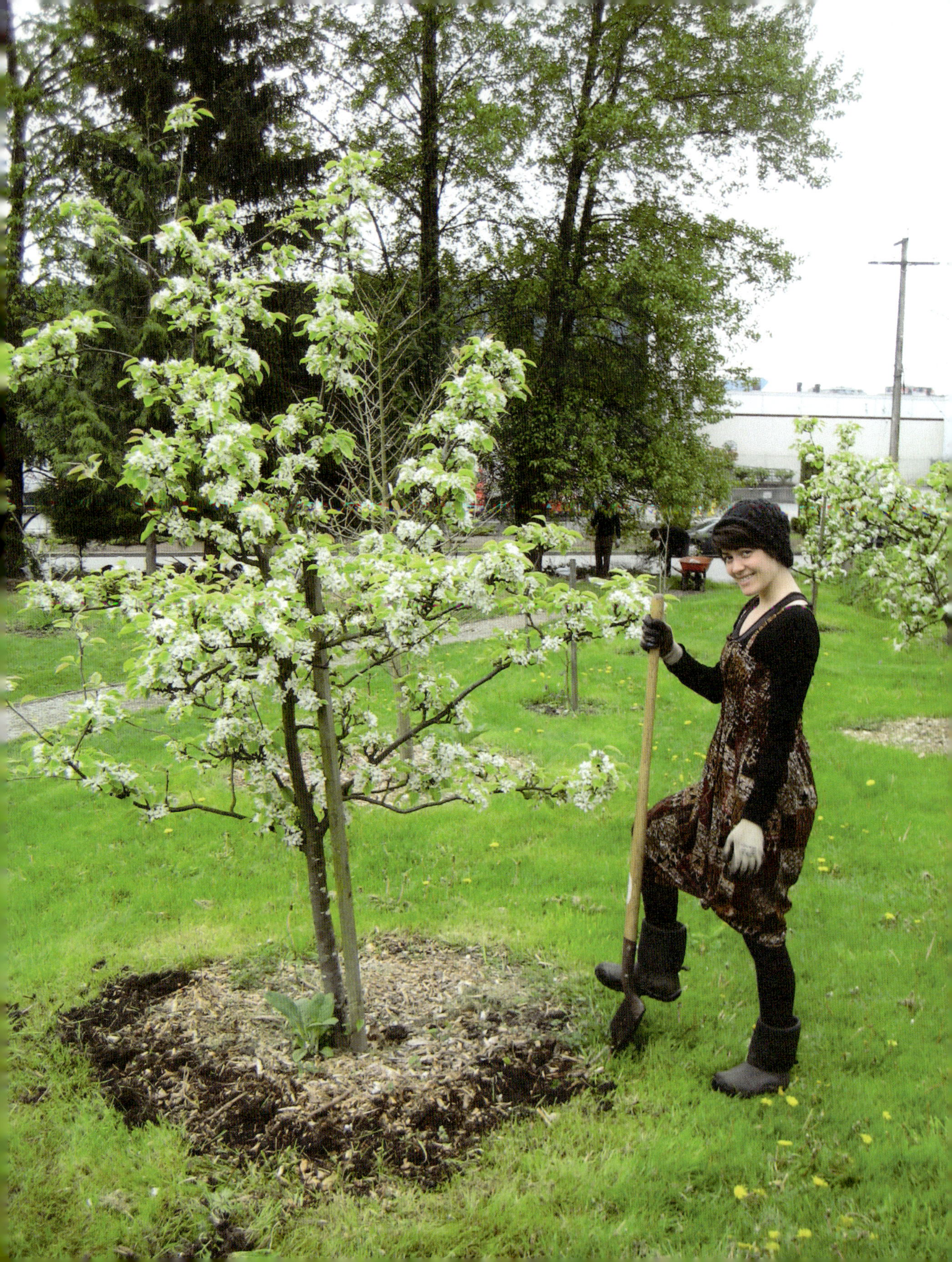

Chapter 5
Planting Your Tree

When you see your first bare root tree, it can be quite shocking. A tree, without dirt protecting its roots, looks so vulnerable. And indeed it is. Bare root trees can be bundled and shipped in the post, if necessary. They are carefully packed to keep their roots moist but not wet. But once they arrive on site in the early spring, they must be planted as soon as possible. Bare root trees can only survive in that state for a short time if they are dormant. Once they "wake up," and their buds start to break, having no soil on their roots will stress and soon kill them.

You can order bare root trees that are a few years old and they'll have branches and may be up to 182 cm (six feet) tall. Younger bare root trees, called "whips," are less expensive and they can be tiny and branchless, looking like a twig with roots. In both cases, there are huge advantages to planting bare root trees. Potted trees are often larger and look better when you buy them, but bare root trees grow more vigorously, adapt to their environment better and, if properly maintained, they are more resistant to infestations and disease.

When we picked up a new bare root apple tree to plant in 2012, it was late in the spring. The weather had started to get warmer, and this two-year-old tree's buds were slightly plump — a sign that it was emerging from dormancy. We couldn't plant the tree right away and so my husband Cliff and I stored it in our garden shed, hoping it would be a bit cooler in there than it would be if we left it out in our sunny yard.

The following day, it was clear immediate planting was expedient. A few of the buds were starting to break open. We carried the tree up to our park and started digging. This was a replacement tree for our orchard, so we knew exactly where to plant it. But when planting a new fruit tree, one of your key considerations will be tree spacing. There are three main considerations:

- Your trees should be close enough to each other to encourage cross-pollination so that the bees and other pollinators can easily fly from tree to tree.

- Your trees should be far enough away from each other so that their roots do not compete for water and nutrition.

- Your trees should be placed such that, when they are mature, with a full canopy, they do not shade each other out.

The rule of thumb is that smaller dwarf trees can be grown 3.5 to 4.5 metres (12 to 15 feet) apart. Semi-dwarf trees will be planted 4.5 to 5.5 metres (15 to 18 feet) apart. And full-size trees will need to be planted up to 8 metres (30 feet) apart.

Planting a Bare Root Tree

Order your bare root tree from a specialist nursery in the summer or fall the year before you want to plant your tree. It will be sent to you in the mail in the early spring. When your tree arrives, plant it as soon as possible. Here is how:

1. Unwrap your bare root tree and soak the roots in a bucket of water for 20 minutes or so while you dig your hole.

2. Dig a hole that is large enough to accommodate the roots fanned out away from the trunk. The hole can be about 90 cm (three feet) wide and about 30 cm (one foot) deep. If your tree has one long root, dig a trench to accommodate it. Do not prune the roots and do not wrap them in circles to fit them in the hole. If you do the latter, the roots will continue to grow in circles and may eventually strangle the growing tree.

3. **Break up the soil** that you removed from the hole and mix in a small amount of triple mix or vegetable-based compost for extra nutrition, but not too much. You want your bare root tree to adapt to the soil it will be growing in.

4. **Pour a bucket of water** into the empty hole. Wait until it drains a bit and then add some more. This will ensure the tree has access to water as soon as it is planted.

5. **Put a shovel across** the hole to give you an idea of where the top of the soil will be. Then have a friend hold the tree up so the graft (which looks like bulge or curve at the bottom of the tree's trunk) is an 2.5-5 cm (one or two inches) above the soil line.

6. **Ensure the roots** are stretched away from the trunk and then carefully backfill the hole so that all the roots are covered. Gently press down the soil with your hands to ensure that there are no large air pockets.

7. **Water your tree** deeply but gently and slowly, with about 4 litres (one gallon) of water that will both irrigate your tree and wash excess soil into air pockets. Focus on the root area and be careful not to splash the trunk of the tree. This is called "watering in."

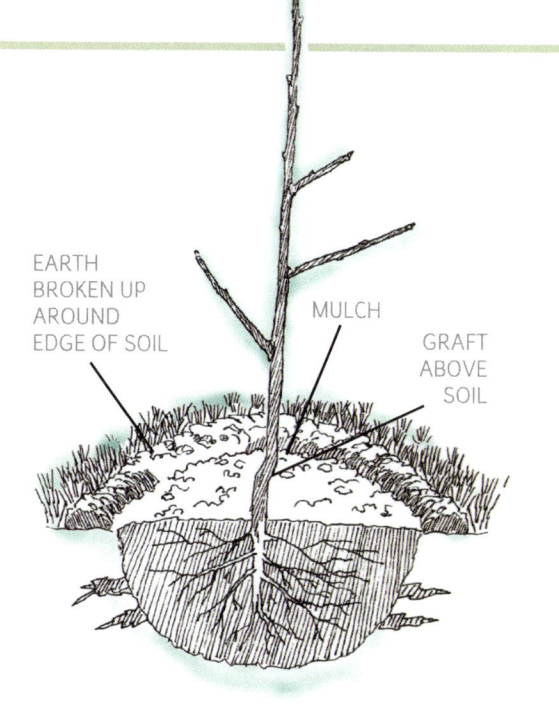

EARTH BROKEN UP AROUND EDGE OF SOIL
MULCH
GRAFT ABOVE SOIL

When planting your fruit tree, ensure the graft union is 2.5-5 cm (one or two inches) above the soil line.

8. **Sprinkle a layer** of compost on top of the dirt for an extra boost of nutrition, and then cover with 7.5 cm (three inches) of mulch in a donut shape, keeping the mulch 12.5 cm (five inches) away from the trunk to protect the trunk from moisture damage.

9. **For the first six weeks** after first planting, water your tree every three or four days until it adapts to its new environment. Then water once or twice a week for the rest of the growing season (reduce watering when natural rainfall occurs). You'll slowly wind down your watering in the early fall to prepare the tree for dormancy.

GROWING URBAN ORCHARDS

"Whipping" the Tree

After planting, mulching and watering a bare root tree there is one more thing you need to do. It's called "whipping" the tree. With one simple pruning cut you encourage your tree to release the hormones it needs to kick-start growth. Not only that, by cutting the whip, you are allowing the tree to devote more energy to developing its root system rather than expanding its canopy. If you don't cut off enough of the top part of the tree, you may have a large tree with immature roots that cannot effectively feed the tree or provide stability.

1. Find a nice healthy bud on the "central leader" of the tree about 122 cm (48 inches) above the ground (for a 9/15-inch caliper trunk tree). If your tree is smaller, you can cut as low as 60 cm (24 inches). For a larger bare root tree you can cut higher up, at about 152 cm (60 inches).

2. Use a clean pair of hand pruners (see Chapter 8) to cut just above that bud. It may feel like you are cutting away most of your tree.

3. Discard the pruned off branches. You may want to even cut them up into small bits and add them to your compost heap. Send your tree lots of love and good wishes for a long, healthy and productive future.. Then your planting job is done for the day.

CUT AFTER PLANTING

Whipping a Tree

Your first pruning cut after planting is "whipping" your fruit tree. Cutting off the top of your young tree spurs vigorous growth in the first months after planting.

Staking a Tree

It's a good idea to stake small trees to ensure visibility and to support the tree in the first two years. Indeed, many types of dwarf trees need permanent staking, as their rootstock cannot support the tree on its own. Ensure your stakes are 61 cm (two feet) taller than your tree, so you can pound them a foot or two into the ground for stability.

1. Pound two 2x2-inch wooden stakes into the ground with a mallet, 15 to 30 cm (six to twelve inches) from each side of the tree. Do not place the stakes too close to the tree, as they can rub off the precious buds, the future architecture of your tree.

2. Take a soft tie (like an old pair of nylons or a piece of rubber hose) and loop it around the stake and the tree from each side. The tie should be supportive but not tight enough to dig into the tree too much or to restrict growth.

Staking Your Tree

Stake your young tree when you plant it to ensure visibility and to support it for the first couple of years.

Planting a Potted Tree

You can only plant bare root trees in the spring. If your goal is to plant your trees in the summer, your only choice is to plant a potted tree. This is easier and more familiar for most of us.

1. Dig a large hole, two or three times the size of your pot. Use a shovel to break up the surface inside the hole to encourage the roots to stretch out into solid ground.

2. Take the tree out of the pot and gently and quickly rough up the outside of the root ball to release some of its roots. Do not spend too much time massaging the roots of your tree, because doing so can damage the microscopic root hairs.

3. Pour some water in the hole, allow it to drain down, and then add some more so that your tree will immediately have access to water.

4. Place the root ball in the hole. Ensure the top of the root ball is in line with the top of the soil, and that the tree's graft (bulge or curve at the bottom of the tree trunk) is an inch or two above the soil line.

5. Take the soil you shoveled out of the hole and use it to backfill the hole. Tamp down with your feet until your tree feels stable and secure.

6. Sprinkle some compost on top of the dirt then cover with 7.5 cm (three inches) of mulch in a donut shape, keeping the mulch 13 cm (five inches) away from the trunk.

7. Water your tree deeply, being careful to sprinkle the water in the trench (the middle of the donut) without splashing the trunk of the tree.

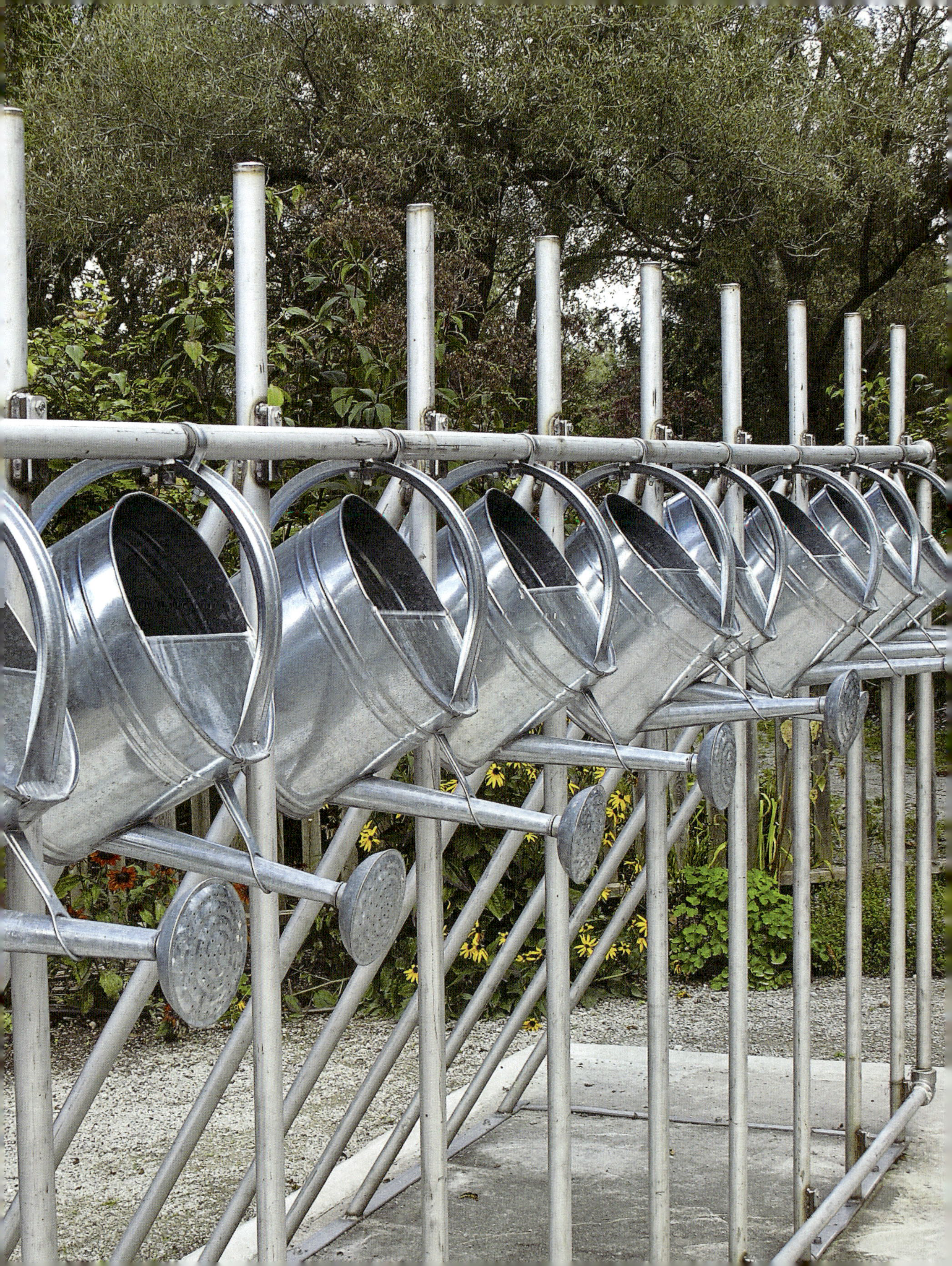

Chapter 6
Caring for Your Trees

The first year that we planted our fruit trees in Ben Nobleman Park, we were keen to see them produce fruit. In fact, some of the trees we purchased from the garden centre already had tiny cherries or pears on them. It would have been so easy to let them grow. Within months we could have our first harvest!

So it was heartbreaking when we learned that, for our young trees to establish themselves properly, it is best to gently remove all of the fruit from the tree for the first two years after planting. Why? If the fruit were allowed to grow to full size, it would snap the fragile young branches. Removing the fruit allows the tree to pour its energy into growing stronger and expanding its root system.

Over the years we have learned that young fruit trees have special needs that are very different from the needs of older trees. While young fruit trees need to be nurtured, more established, older trees just need to be maintained. In this section I will outline they key elements of fruit tree care for younger and more mature trees.

Young Tree Care

Young trees need to be nurtured for the first two or three years until they settle into their new location. These are the key tasks involved in caring for young trees:

Watering

Young trees need to be watered every few days for the first six weeks after planting. After that, you can water young trees once a week (twice a week when the weather is really hot and dry). Watering usually starts in May and goes through to the end of September. No watering is necessary in the winter, when the tree is dormant. It's also not necessary in the early spring, when the snow is melting and rain is plentiful.

Watering Tips

- Water your trees deeply with about three buckets of water per tree.
- The amount of water each tree needs depends on the type of soil it is planted in. Sandy soil may need more than three buckets of water. Clay soil may need less.
- Water slowly and pause often to make sure the water is being absorbed. Stop watering if standing puddles form around the tree.
- Focus the water on the feeder roots of your tree located in the soil under the tree's canopy and dripline.
- Keep the water away from the trunk, branches and leaves of your tree, in order to avoid rotting the wood and to prevent the spread of waterborne diseases.
- Do not overwater, as too much water can cause fungal disease or root rot.

Tools:
- One-gallon bucket
- Screwdriver
- Water

Procedure:

1. Pierce three holes in the bottom of your bucket with the screwdriver – if necessary, pound the screwdriver in with a hammer or mallet.

2. Place the bucket under the canopy of your young tree but not too close to the trunk.

3. Use your hose to fill the bucket with water. Allow the water to slowly drain out.

4. When the bucket is empty, move it to another location under the tree's canopy and refill it with water. Allow it to drain.

5. Move the bucket a third time to another location under the canopy, refill it and allow it to drain again.

The Leaky Bucket Technique

This is a cheap and cheerful irrigation technique that works well. While you wait for your buckets to drain, you can always weed around the tree or do other garden work.

Installing a Drip Irrigation System

Alternatively, if you want your irrigation system to be automated, you can set up an inexpensive irrigation system using a timer and drip irrigation hoses purchased from your local garden centre. This works well if you're planting your fruit trees at a cottage and you want to ensure that they get water throughout the week.

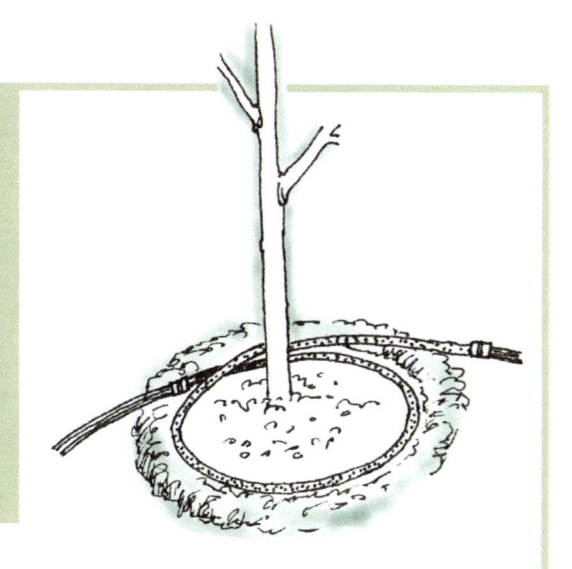

Tools:
- Regular hose
- Soaker hose
- Landscape fabric staples
- Pounder (to pound in the landscape fabric staples)
- Water timer
- Number of hose menders

Procedure:

1. Measure the distance from your garden tap to your tree. Ensure your regular hose is long enough to go that distance.

2. Attach the water timer to your tap and attach your regular hose to the timer.

3. Spread the hose out towards your tree and, if necessary, secure the hose in the soil as you go along with landscape fabric staples, to ensure it won't move around.

4. Once you are two feet from your tree, cut your regular hose and use a hose mender to attach it to the beginning of your soaker hose.

5. Circle your soaker hose around your tree's trunk (twice or more is good to ensure all of the roots get access to water), ensuring that it is at least one foot away from the actual trunk of the tree. Anchor your hose in place with landscape fabric staples.

6. If this is your only tree, you can attach a hose ender there. If you want the irrigation system to continue on to other trees, attach more sections of regular and soaker hoses as necessary to ensure all the trees are watered and then attach your hose ender.

7. Test the water to ensure your tap is on. Then set the timer to water your young trees for an hour once or twice a week or as necessary, depending on the tree's age and the weather conditions.

8. Cover your soaker hose with mulch to help keep the moisture in the soil.

9. As winter approaches, you will need to detach the regular hose sections of your system. Number the pieces with a permanent marker so you know where to reinstall them next year. Store them in your shed. The soaker hose sections are porous, so it's safe to leave them in the garden over the winter.

- Do not use a sprinkler system. They may be handy, but sprinklers soak the tree as well as the roots and can cause the wood to rot or become diseased.
- You can water your trees with an old-fashioned watering can if you have the patience. Or try one of the two simple watering techniques on page 42 and 43.

Feeding

Fruit trees aren't really so different from humans. If we don't have nutritious food to eat, we will not thrive. The same goes for fruit trees. Once they've consumed the nutrition that is available in the soil, they need an alternative source of nutrients. Being rooted to the ground means they don't have the flexibility that humans and animals have in being able to move to another location to forage for food. And if you planted your tree in poor soil in the first place, it will have a rough start to life.

That's why it's helpful to mix a small amount of good quality compost into your soil before you first plant your tree, and why we add up to 5 cm (two inches) of quality compost or well rotted manure onto the soil above your tree's roots as a top dressing each spring thereafter. With time and rain, the nutrients will sink into the earth and be accessible to the tree's roots. The nutrition will give our trees a burst of energy that will help them grow throughout the summer. It is not wise to feed your trees in the fall, as that will give them energy at a time when they should be getting ready for dormancy over the winter months. For more details read Chapter 7 on soil.

Mulching

Early spring is also a good time to mulch your trees, as mulch helps suppress weeds and helps keep moisture near the tree's roots. It also protects your trees from lawnmowers and string trimmers, which can injure your tree if they get too close. Place your mulch in a ring, or donut shape, around the tree's trunk, but it must not touch the trunk at all. If the tree was mulched from the previous year, pull back the mulch, add the compost, move the mulch back on top of the compost, and add fresh mulch as necessary to maintain five cm (two inches) of compressed, settled mulch around the tree at all times.

Removing the Baby Fruit

For the first two years you will need to remove ALL the baby fruit from your trees so that the tree will pour its energy into developing its roots. This is especially important with plum trees. They produce a lot of fruit, and if it is allowed to mature when the tree is young, the fruit could break the tree's fragile young branches.

Pruning

Pruning at least once a year, usually in the early spring while the tree is dormant, is very important as a way to create a solid structure for the tree. Correct pruning can promote good air circulation and will help give all the branches equal access to sunlight so the tree can produce enough glucose, through photosynthesis, to feed itself and store extra sugar where we want it: in the fruit. When done properly, pruning also gives your tree energy, helps combat disease and generally improves tree health. For more instructions see Chapter 8 on pruning.

Weeding

Weeding tends to be an afterthought when it comes to planting fruit trees. Somehow, many of us feel that our young trees can tolerate weeds because they are slightly bigger than the weeds around them. In truth, fruit trees do not compete well with weeds, especially the ones that hog water and nutrients like dandelion, vetch and even grass. In Ben Nobleman Park, we weed our trees every two weeks during the growing season. Picking a few weeds now prevents a buildup of weeds later, and allows our trees to enjoy any nutrients and water in the soil without having to share them with other plants.

Mouse Guards

In some areas, there are small animals, like mice or rabbits, which like to nibble on fruit tree bark. You can prevent that from happening by putting a plastic mouse guard on your tree for the first two or three years (you can remove it in the summer). Often the trees will come with a mouse guard, a white piece of plastic coiled around the trunk. Just ensure that it isn't so tight that it is restricting the growth of the tree's trunk. Before the winter, you may also want to pull back the mulch around your tree to ensure that mice don't make a nice nest in there and then start nibbling on your young tree's delicate bark as a mid-winter snack.

Mature Tree Care

You will mulch and add compost to your trees every year (especially at your trees constantly expanding drip-line, where the feeder roots are growing), no matter how old they are or how many years since they were planted. Also continue to prune your trees annually. But two main factors change once your tree is older and well established: irrigation and thinning the fruit.

Irrigation for Older Trees

Once a tree is established and its roots, including its feeder roots, have spread out far and wide, it needs less assistance in accessing water. Mature trees still do need watering, especially during a hot, dry spell in the middle of summer. But as your trees get older, you'll be able to space out irrigation sessions more — perhaps every three weeks or once a month. Remember that a deep watering is always more useful than watering lightly.

Thinning the Fruit on Older Trees

By year three, you can allow your trees to fruit. Still, many trees, like plums, for example, produce much more fruit than their branches can handle. Often trees provide their own solution to this and it's called "June drop." In June (or sometimes July), many fruit trees will spontaneously drop a lot of excess baby fruit. This is nature's way of getting rid of substandard

---

Correct pruning can promote good air circulation

Thinning the Fruit

BEFORE HAND THINNING APPLES ARE IN CLUSTERS

AFTER HAND THINNING APPLES ARE ABOUT 80 CM (SIX INCHES) APART

fruit, leaving behind a smaller amount that it can realistically maintain.

After June drop, we help the tree even more by judiciously thinning out the fruit that remains. We do this for two reasons. First of all, the remaining fruit will be healthier and sweeter since the tree's energy will not be spread so thinly. Also you are ensuring that two adjacent apples, for instance, will not crowd each other out, each preventing the other from growing to full size.

When it comes to apricots, if your tree is packed with fruit that doesn't fall off during June drop, you may want to thin it out anyway to protect the tree branches from breaking under the weight and to ensure that each piece of fruit has the space to grow to full size. So how do you thin? Often, fruit trees grow their fruit in clusters. After June drop, choose just one baby fruit in each cluster to keep, and then gently remove the rest. In apples, it is often the largest fruit – also known as the "king fruit," which is believed to have the best genetics of the bunch – that is retained. Then think about the size of the fruit once it's full-grown, and ensure that you have that amount of space, anywhere from 12 to 20 cm (5 to 8 inches) between the remaining young fruits.

Fruits that Benefit from Hand Thinning:
- Apples
- Pears
- Asian pears
- Plums
- Peaches

Other Types of Fruit Trees do Well Without Thinning:
- Sweet cherries
- Sour cherries
- Apricots

Orchard Inspiration: The Sharing Farm Society, Richmond B.C.

Mary Gazetas, a woman of great energy and passion, wanted to make organic food accessible to all. So in 2001, she and a group of volunteers launched The Richmond Fruit Tree Sharing Project. Their goal was to harvest excess fruit from local residential fruit trees to donate to the needy. The project was a huge success, and the group donated hundreds of pounds of fruit to the food bank in the early years.

Soon Mary and the others acquired the right to use city land to grow organic vegetables and fruit trees. Today, The Sharing Farm cultivates a five-acre vegetable farm and a 1.5-acre orchard of more than 400 fruit trees, and they supply thousands of pounds of produce to the foodbank each year.

The orchard itself proved to be an opportunity to learn, and The Sharing Farm has offered fruit tree care workshops led by pomologist and sustainable agriculture specialist Kent Mullinix, Ph.D. In 2010, the Sharing Farms orchard became the host location for the Richmond Farm School, a 10-month-long course organized by Kwantlen Polytechnic University. As part of this course, the students spend 80 hours learning how to grow fruit.

Kimi Hendess, orchard manager for The Sharing Farm Society, says each year they learn more about how to care for their trees.

Her advice to aspiring orchardists is:

*Assess your resources before you plant your trees. Once you plant a tree, it has many time-sensitive needs. It needs watering, pruning and horticultural management, nitrogen at the right time, and good soil fertility. Make sure you know who will do this work and how it will be funded.

*Start small … that might mean 25 trees, it might mean 10 trees, or it might mean three trees depending on who you are and what space you have. But don't be afraid to start. Try it and learn as you go. Over a three- to five-year period, you will know if you have the resources to expand.

*Find an experienced mentor who is willing to give advice throughout the season, help you identify pests and diseases, and help identify priorities and the schedule of operations.

In 2012, sadly, Mary Gazetas passed away at the age of 68. But her legacy continues to grow along with the fruit trees in The Sharing Farm's Orchard.

"Mary was a real visionary," says Kimi. "She made things happen. She inspired people to get involved. Mary was a rock and we all really miss her, but her legacy lives on and we farm with her vision strong in our hearts."

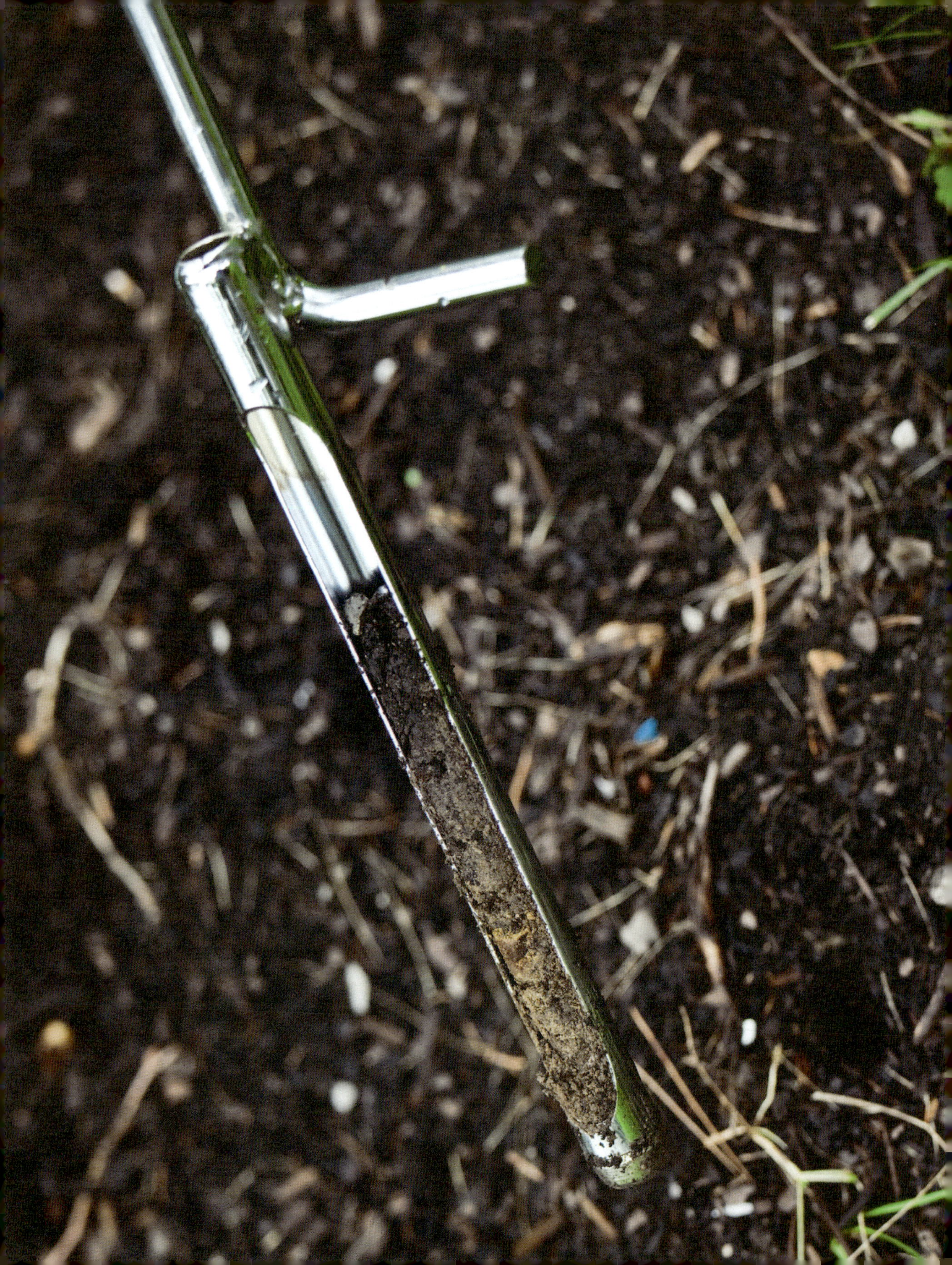

Chapter 7
Feeding Your Trees

Gardeners from Toronto's Parks, Forestry and Recreation department helped us plant our first nine fruit trees in June, 2009. It was late in the season, so we planted potted trees rather than bare root. On planting day, our young potted trees looked good. They had developed leaves during their time in the nursery and some even had baby fruit.

You'd think the trees would thrive after being moved from a pot into a nice permanent location in a park. But six weeks after the trees were planted, they were not thriving. A healthy young fruit tree can grow 46 to 61 cm (18 to 24 inches) a year. We should have seen 10 to 15 cm (four to six inches) of growth on our trees by then. Instead, the soft burgundy-coloured shoots at the end of our tree's branches were hardly 2.5 cm (one inch) long. One of our Parks and Recreation contacts came to have a look.

"They need more nitrogen," he said. I wasn't exactly sure what that meant.

Years later, it all seems so obvious to me. If you buy a tank and some goldfish, you know you have to feed them regularly. Once they finish their food, those fish can't just hop out of their tank and forage for more food. It's similar for fruit trees. Once they consume the food near their roots, they can't go for a stroll to find some more nutrition in a different location. And yet, when we plant young trees, we often assume that they can fend for themselves.

Once a tree is established, it is more independent. Trees use sunlight to convert carbon dioxide and water into carbohydrates. Their roots extract water and essential nutrients from the soil and they transport those nutrients up into the various parts of the tree. But what if the soil a tree is planted in isn't nutrient-rich? That's the case with much of the soil you'll find in an urban environment. To understand why, we need to examine what soil is.

What is Soil?

Soil is the medium in which plants and trees grow. It is made up of a number of layers. The top layer, called topsoil, is the most fertile, and it is made up of organic (once living) materials such as decaying plants and animals mixed together with inorganic (non-living) materials like rock or minerals. Soil also contains air and water and is home to millions of insects and micro-organisms which play an essential role in keeping the soil healthy. A healthy layer of topsoil might be 20 cm (eight inches) thick or more.

Underneath the topsoil you will find subsoil. We see subsoil all the time on building sites, because one of the first steps when building a new home is to strip away and remove the valuable topsoil, which may then be packaged and sold. Subsoil is hard and lighter in colour than topsoil. It has very little organic material. Fewer plants and animals can survive in this layer of soil. Beneath the subsoil there is a layer of weathered rock, which is predominantly inhospitable to plant or animal life.

In an urban environment, there are few green spaces that haven't been disturbed at some point to make way for building and development. Once the building work is done, a small amount of topsoil is then shipped in to cover the subsoil, and grass is often planted on top. Imported topsoil and grass don't provide the same rich growing environment that undisturbed topsoil, teeming with life and rich in biodiversity, would have. That's why urban orchardists and gardeners have an uphill struggle when it comes to improving their soil.

Not only are our trees planted in poor soil, they also don't enjoy the benefits of the cycles of nature. In the wilderness, nutritious organic matter is constantly added to the soil as leaves and branches fall to the ground and slowly decay, and dead plants and insects

Spreading quality compost around the base of a young tree in our park.

The best way to get to know your soil is to go outside and feel it

decompose. But in our gardens we rush to clean up the fallen leaves and branches. We remove dead plants and animals. Once our trees have absorbed any nutrition in their soil, the feast is over and famine begins.

Urban orchardists need to work hard just to get their soil up to an adequate level of health, and we can do that simply and efficiently with a soil test and by judiciously applying organic amendments. That, together with adding compost and mulch to our trees annually, will allow our trees to be healthy and productive for years to come.

Assessing Your Soil

Before testing your soil, it's good to get to know it a little bit. Is it dry and sandy? It is wet and waterlogged? Is it crumbly, porous and absorbent? The best way to get to know your soil is to go outside and feel it. Here's an easy way to evaluate your soil's texture.

Soil Texture

On a day when your soil is moist but not wet, dig up a handful of soil from the earth near your trees with a trowel. Then take the soil in your hand and try to press it into a ball.

Does your soil stay in a ball in your hand? If so, you have clay soil. Clay is made up of tiny particles that stick together. Clay can be good because it is often rich in nutrients. The downside is that heavy clay can be dense, making it hard for roots to move through as they search for water and nutrients. Heavy clay can also have poor drainage, resulting in water collecting around the tree in swampy puddles. Fruit trees growing in poorly drained soil are vulnerable to root and fungal diseases.

Does your soil crumble in small chunks and pieces? If so, you have silty soil. Silt particles are larger than clay and so there are more tiny air pockets between particles. If you have silty soil, you're lucky. This type of soil allows tree roots to easily expand and push their way through.

Does your soil fall apart and run through your fingers? Sandy soil is made up of very large particles, 100 times larger than silt particles and 1,000 times larger than clay. The downside of sandy soil is that it is often nutrient-deficient and it doesn't retain water well at all, making it hard for your tree's roots in the upper surface of the soil to access the water they need for the tree to survive.

Soil pH and Nutrients

While you can learn a lot about your soil by feeling it, it's harder to determine other soil characteristics. Is the soil acidic or alkaline? What level of nutrients does it have? These are the main factors a soil test will reveal.

Orchard Inspiration: Strathcona Community Garden, Vancouver, B.C.

Having one or two fruit trees in your yard involves some work. But imagine having 300 fruit trees in your community garden. That's the case with the Strathcona Community Garden in Vancouver, British Columbia. Members of this garden group, who pay just $15 a year to tend one of Strathcona's 200 garden plots, share the responsibilities of caring for the communal trees. The first fruit trees were planted on the site in 1987, so Strathcona has many mature trees offering an abundant harvest.

Strathcona's gardeners spend most of their time working on their own garden plots, growing flowers or vegetables. But on the last Sunday of every month, all members are expected to participate in a work party followed by a potluck meal. That's when they care for communal assets. They maintain pathways, turn the compost pile and mulch, prune and fertilize the fruit trees. At harvest time, they divide up and share the harvest.

Getting more than 100 gardeners, all with different levels of fruit-tree care experience, to take a unified approach to managing the trees can be a challenge. The trees, though they do suffer from pest and disease problems, are never sprayed. Pruning techniques are not always consistent. But one thing Strathcona's gardeners always do is fertilize their trees each spring.

David Tracey, an arborist, writer and member of the community garden, says they ensure that their trees have access to a wide variety of nutrients by alternating fertilizers.

"Every year we add our own home-made compost and in the spring we always use some sort of organic fertilizer. If we use composted horse manure one year, we will switch to composted chicken manure another year or composted sheep manure. We don't test the soil like many orchards do, but it seems to work out because our trees are growing well."

Among the most beautiful parts of Strathcona's orchard are the espaliered fruit trees. These are trees that are trained to grow along fences, an approach that makes it easier to grow a large number of fruit trees in a small space. The espaliered trees are mostly heirloom apples, but in other parts of the garden they grow Asian pears, cherries, plums and nut trees, and they are even experimenting with pawpaws, an exotic-tasting fruit from a tree that is native to parts of Canada.

Tracey, who has written a number of books on urban agriculture, is keen to see others plant fruit trees, whether in their gardens or in a common space:

"Do it! Plant fruit trees! It's a good idea. Do it and learn on the job," he says.

Espaliered fruit trees are grown on fences in Strathcona Community Gardens.

Acidic or Alkaline

Some soils are acidic, some are alkaline and most are somewhere in between. PH is measured on a scale from zero to 14, with zero being very acidic and 14 being extremely alkaline. If your soil is below 6.0, it is acidic. If it's above 7.0, it's alkaline. Most fruit trees thrive in the range of 6.0 to 6.5. Blueberries prefer more acidic soil, in the range of 4.5 to 5.5. It's important to get the pH balance of your soil right, because when it is too acidic or alkaline, tree roots cannot access the nutrients in the soil

Primary Nutrients

There are the three primary nutrients that we need in our soil in order for our fruit trees to thrive:

Nitrogen (N)

Nitrogen promotes leafy growth. Trees need it in the right amount. If you add too much, the tree will pour lots of energy into leaf and branch growth while producing fewer flowers and fruits. There are organic nitrogen-rich fertilizers including composted animal manures, bloodmeal and alfalfa meal.

Phosphorus (P)

This nutrient helps trees develop strong root systems. It can be found in large amounts in bonemeal or rock phosphate. Sandy soils are often phosphorus-deficient, making it difficult for fruit trees to settle in well without amended soil.

Potassium (K)

Potassium helps trees fight disease and improves the quality of the fruit on your trees. Sandy soil low in organic matter will often be potassium-deficient. Animal manure (from chickens, cows and sheep) has lots of potassium as well. You can also boost potassium levels by adding seaweed meal.

Secondary Nutrients and Micronutrients

The three secondary nutrients that are needed in smaller amounts of healthy soil are calcium, sulphur and magnesium. Fruit trees also need very small amounts of micronutrients including boron, copper, chlorine, iron, manganese, molybdenum and zinc.

In general, there are three aspects to soil care for orchards. They involve mulching and adding organic matter, adding nitrogen annually, and soil testing and amending.

N-P-K Labels

As you learn more about improving your soil with organic amendments, you will start to pay attention to the N-P-K numbers listed on the packaging of the products at your garden centre. This number represents the ratio of nitrogen (N), phosphorous (P) and potassium (K), in that order, and can help you choose a product that suits your needs. So 6-2-0 will be six percent nitrogen, 2 percent phosphorus and 2 percent potassium, for instance. More about that later on, when we talk about the various organic supplements available for fruit growers.

Alfalfa hay is a nutritious mulch that can be spread on top of the roots of your fruit trees.

Mulching and Adding Organic Matter

Mulching and adding organic matter to your soil is a no-brainer. Just as you'd feed the fish in your fish tank daily, you will be adding organic matter (like compost or well-rotted manure) and mulch to your trees annually in the early spring. This will ensure your trees will have nutrition for the growing season.

Some orchardists add extra mulch in the fall as a way of preparing their trees for a cold winter. But it is important to remember not to add compost or well-rotted manure in the fall. That's sort of like giving a child chocolates at bedtime. The fall is the time for the tree to go into dormancy, and adding nutrition at that time of year will give your tree an energy boost that will delay dormancy and that can be unhealthy for your tree.

Here are the key amendments we use regularly:

Compost

(1-1-1 or variable depending on the quality of your compost):

Good compost is a miracle amendment. Not only does it contain small amounts of the N-P-K nutrients that will slowly release into your soil, but it can also help you correct your soil's pH balance. It can make clay soils more friable (crumbly rather than solid like clay) and can give more body and nutrition to sandy soil. Adding compost each spring will do your trees, and your soil, a world of good. And if you are preparing a new site for planting, spread up to 13 cm (five inches) of compost on top of the soil, till it in and then leave it to settle in for a month or more. This will make your site very hospitable for tree planting. You can make your own compost from kitchen scraps, leaves and organic material, or you can purchase it from a garden centre. Make your own compost if you can; it will be much more nutritious than any compost that you can buy in a bag.

Well-Rotted Manure

(2-0-0 for rotted cow manure or variable depending on the quality and source of manure):

Manure also contains the N-P-K nutrients and is sometimes an even more concentrated source. The problem is that fresh manure is potent stuff and if you add it to the soil around your trees you may burn your tree roots. Fresh manure can also contain pathogens that are toxic to humans. That's why we only add well rotted or composted manure to fruit trees, and we add it in small amounts. Rich in organic materials, manure can help pH balance and soil texture. Types of composted or rotted manure available in garden centres include sheep, cow, chicken and turkey manure.

Mulch

There are many different types of mulches. Most of them break down slowly over the years, adding nitrogen and other nutrients to the soil as they break down. Examples include wood bark, wood chips or alfalfa hay. In addition to adding nutrients to the soil, mulches help retain moisture and can prevent weeds from growing around the tree, and they can insulate your tree's roots over the winter and keep the soil cooler in the summer.

In addition to adding nutrients to the soil, mulches help retain moisture and can prevent weeds

Because organic mulches decompose, orchardists need to add more each year. Some avoid this by mulching with pea gravel, which does not break down quickly. Pea gravel doesn't add much organic material to your soil but it does discourage mice from nibbling on your trees and can work well as a way to suppress weeds.

Which Mulch is Best for Your Trees?

In conventional landscape design, gardeners opt for long-lasting mulches that don't break down easily because their main goal is to suppress weeds. When we are growing fruit trees, the suppression of weeds is a secondary goal. Our primary goal is to add the type of mulch that breaks down quickly and adds nutrients to the soil.

Which Mulches Break Down Quickly?

Consider the level of lignin in the product. Lignin is a chemical compound deposited in the cell walls of many plants that makes the plants rigid and woody. Lower lignin mulches are better for fruit trees. So the best mulches will be on the right side of the chart below.

If we go with the conventional high lignin mulches that landscapers often use, we may encounter problems. As the higher lignin mulches such as pine or cedar mulch break down, they actually absorb small amounts of nitrogen from the soil. So a tree mulched with those products may exhibit symptoms of nitrogen deficiency, such as yellowing leaves. This stresses the tree and means it will have less energy to focus on growing, protecting itself from pests and disease, and producing a good harvest.

Adding Nitrogen

You can mulch and add organic matter to your tree starting from the day that you plant it in the ground. In the first year, it is not necessary to add extra nitrogen to the soil. The tree will take that year to get adjusted to its new environment. Let it settle in.

But after your tree has been in the ground for a year, it's time to add nitrogen. Fruit trees consume a lot of nitrogen. Compost and mulch have low levels of nitrogen, and do not supply enough to sustain a young fruit tree. There are other organically acceptable ways of adding nitrogen to the soil around our trees.

Nitrogen and New Growth?

Choose and inspect one branch that extends out of your tree's trunk. You will notice that most of the branch looks woody and brown. But at the end the branch will be softer and more flexible. It may be burgundy coloured or green rather than brown. That is the new growth on your tree.

MORE LIGNIN			LESS LIGNIN
Pine/Cedar Mulch	Hardwood Bark, Cocobean Mulch	Alfalfa Hay	Alfalfa Meal

How to Add Organic Matter and Mulch Your Trees

The goal when adding organic matter and mulching your trees is to ensure there is a layer of compost or well composted manure in a circle on top of your tree's roots and then another layer of mulch on top that is five cm (two inches) thick once it settles. Your mulch circle will start 15 cm (six inches) away from the tree trunk and stretch out to the dripline of the tree.

Tools:
- Shovel
- Mulching fork
- Compost or well-rotted manure
- Mulch

Timing:
- Early spring to mid summer. (Do not add nutrients closer to the fall when the trees are preparing for dormancy.)

Procedure:

1. **Pull back** any existing mulch around your tree.

2. **Add up to five cm (two inches)** of compost or just one inch of well-rotted manure in a circle around the base of your tree.

3. **Focus** the nutrients on the area where the feeder roots are by starting your compost circle 15 cm (six inches) away from the tree trunk and stretching it out to the dripline of the tree.

4. **Put the old mulch** back on top of the compost or well-rotted manure and add more mulch on top as necessary to ensure there is 5 cm (two inches) of compressed mulch in a donut around each tree.

5. **Water** the tree deeply, focusing on the feeder root area so that the nutrition in the compost or manure starts to work its way down into the soil.

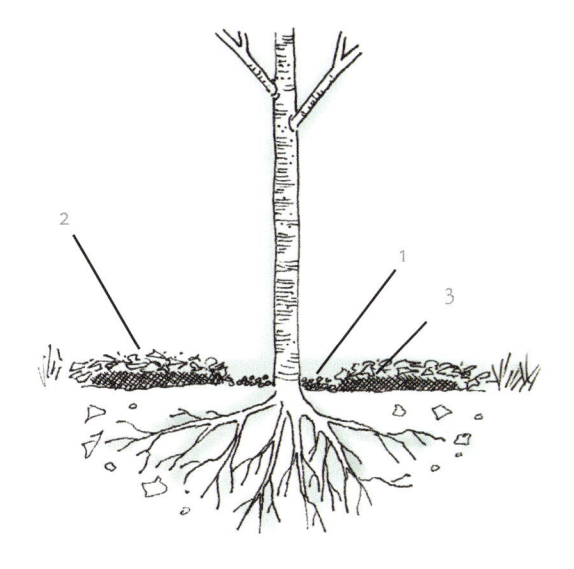

Ensure the compost and mulch does not touch your trees trunk.
1. Ground level bare soil
2. Mulch
3. Compost

GROWING URBAN ORCHARDS

Does the whole branch look soft and flexible? If that's the case, you may have planted a whip that had no branches and so all the growth, starting from where the branch connects with the trunk, is new growth.

How Much Nitrogen Does Your Tree Need?

Now that you know what the new growth looks like you can do your analysis. Take a tape measure and check how many centimetres (inches) of new growth there is on your tree. It should be similar from branch to branch so use a single branch for your measurement. Then look at the estimates below to see how your tree is doing:

- In years one and two you should have approximately 61 cm (24 inches) of new growth each year on each branch.
- In year three and onward you should have from 41 cm (16 inches) to 51 cm (20 inches) of new growth a year on each branch.

The amount of growth you can see will depend on what time of year it is. In early spring, you will be able to see all of last year's growth. After that, you would expect on a tree in year one to see a proportional amount of growth as the season goes on. The chart on page 59 illustrates how that works. This is an estimate that works for apples, pears, cherries and apricots. Plum, peach and nectarine trees are more vigorous growers and they may have even more new growth than this.

Now Do Your Analysis

So let's say you are inspecting your tree in the early spring where you can see all of last year's growth:

- Do you have a tree that's been in the ground for one year and has 60 cm (24 inches) of growth? Great, you don't need to add extra nitrogen.
- Do you have a tree that's been in the ground for one year and has 35 cm (14 inches) of growth? Well, you need to add a modest amount of nitrogen.
- Do you have a tree that's been in the ground for one year and has five cm (two inches) of growth? Then your tree needs the full amount of nitrogen outlined on the package.

Remember, when adding nitrogen-rich products, more is not always better. Too much nitrogen can prevent fruiting and flowering and can burn the roots of your tree. Always read the package carefully and, when in doubt, err on the side of caution.

What Products Can You Use to Add Nitrogen

At the garden centre, you will not find a product that is 100 percent nitrogen. Instead you will choose one of a handful of natural, organically acceptable products that are nitrogen-rich but contain other nutrients as well. All will have their N-P-K rating on the packaging so you can see what percentage of nitrogen (N) the product contains. So if the product is 12-1-0, it has 12 percent nitrogen, one percent phosphorus, and no potassium. Here are a few of the products you can choose from:

Fishmeal

(9-3-0) This is fish essence and it is very useful in young orchards when the trees aren't growing quickly enough. It releases nitrogen slowly over time. The downside? In an urban environment it may attract raccoons, as it did in our garden.

Evaluating Tree Growth to Determine Nitrogen Needs

TIME OF YEAR	EARLY SPRING	LATE SPRING	EARLY SUMMER	LATE SUMMER	EARLY FALL
How much growth to expect in a tree in years 1 and 2	61 cm (24 inches) based at last year's growth	15 cm (6 inches) based on this year's growth	30 cm (12 inches) based on this year's growth	46 cm (18 inches) based on this year's growth	61 cm (24 inches) based on this year's growth
How much growth to expect in a tree in year 3	51 cm (20 inches) based on last year's growth	13 cm (5 inches) based on this year's growth	25 cm (10 inches) based on this year's growth	38 cm (15 inches) based on this year's growth	51 cm (20 inches) based on this year's growth

You might consider applying it a good few hours before a rain so that the product dries first, and then is washed into the soil.

Alfalfa Meal

(2-1-2) This is a plant-based source of nitrogen. In our orchard, we mulched our trees with alfalfa hay, which would eventually break down and add nitrogen to our soil. The meal releases nitrogen more quickly and works well to give fruit trees a mid-summer boost.

Organic Fertilizer Blends

(N-P-K will be written on the packaging). These concoctions can be made with a mix of natural products including nitrogen meals, rock phosphates and more. Some are designed to support wood growth in younger trees and others support fruiting. Make sure the blend has a high N value compared to P and K, and read the packaging well before use.

Blood Meal

(12-0-0) Many organic growers use bloodmeal to add nitrogen to their soil because, as you can see from the NPK number, which indicates 12 percent nitrogen content, you can add less of it to give your tree the nutritional boost it needs. Bloodmeal is a powder byproduct of the meat industry that is made out of the dried blood of cows or other animals. The main downside is that it may attract dogs and raccoons so consider applying it before it rains.

How to Apply Nitrogen

All of these products will have detailed instructions on the packaging. Be sure to read them carefully, as adding too much nitrogen can burn the roots of your tree. Some products tell you to add a tablespoon of the powdered product per square foot. And they will outline how frequently you must do this.

Other products may give you a total amount of product to add per tree annually. So let's say they suggest you add a pound of the product on your tree each year. In that case, you will divide that number into three and plan three separate applications, each time adding 1/3 of a pound around your tree. The applications should start in the early spring, before flowering. The second application should take place a month after that. And the third application should take place a month after the second application.

So, for instance, if your apricots blossom in early May, you can do your first application on April 20. The next application will be on May 20 and the final application will be on June 20.

Do not add any type of nitrogen-rich product after mid-summer as it can damage your tree by delaying dormancy. Instead, wait until next year and apply it in the early spring.

Soil Testing

If you add organic matter and nitrogen each year, you are on your way to having a well-tended tree. The third key to having healthy soil

How to Take a Soil Sample

Before you take your soil sample, decide where you will have your soil tested. Different labs have different requirements, so be sure to read their instructions on how much soil to send in before taking your sample. Then take your sample when the soil is dry and ensure that the tools, bucket and bag you use are clean. Do not use tools made of galvanized metal as they are coated with zinc and can skew test results.

Tools:
- Spade
- Trowel
- Bucket
- Sandwich-sized plastic bag or another type of bag supplied by your lab

Procedure:

1. Use your spade to dig five holes on your site that are 20 to 30 cm (8 to 12 inches) deep.

2. Use your spade to cut a 1.5-cm (half-inch) slice of soil from the side each of hole.

3. Put each of these thin slices into your bucket.

4. Use your trowel to mix the contents of the bucket thoroughly.

5. Scoop the amount of soil required by your lab (it's usually two cups) from the bucket into a clean sandwich-sized bag.

6. Fill out the form supplied by your lab requesting the type of test that you want.

7. Place your bag of soil into a small box for shipping, enclose the form, send it to the lab for testing and wait for the result.

is to have your soil tested. Organic orchardists test their soil every few years and each time they amend the soil because they realize that a healthy tree provides better harvests and is more resistant to pests and disease. This is even more important in an urban environment where the soil quality is poor and salt damage is common.

Your can test your soil in the spring or in the fall. Then add your amendments once you get your results. The amendments will then have time to work their way into the soil before the summer season. If you can, test and amend your soil a year before planting your first trees to ensure they are planted into a nutrient-rich environment.

Working with Your Local Soil Testing Lab

On page 60, I explain how to take a soil sample which you can send to a local soil testing lab. Ask for a test that measures pH balance, phosphorus and potassium, as well as the secondary nutrients and micronutrients, and, since fruit trees have their own unique requirements, explain that you will be planting fruit trees. (Nitrogen levels fluctuate during the year, so the nitrogen reading may not be very helpful.)

If you ask for a simple report, you may receive a report with numbers on it that you don't understand. Often you can pay a little extra to ensure that the lab will include concrete recommendations about how to correct your soil. Most often labs are testing soil for farmers with large holdings, so their recommendations are written up in terms of pounds of product per acre. Ask the lab to adjust the results to a small garden. Instead of prescribing soil amendments in terms of pounds per acre, they can adapt the number to pounds per 1,000 square feet.

If you do get a pounds-per-acre recommendation, divide the figure by 43 to get pounds per 1,000 square feet and if you have any questions, call the lab for advice rather than taking a chance and applying fertilizers that you do not need.

Choosing Amendments

Once you receive your test result recommendations, you can bring them to your local garden centre and ask a qualified staff member to suggest organic products to use. All registered fertilizers come with a N-P-K number like 6-2-0 or 5-3-3. This number represents the ratio of nitrogen (N), phosphorous (P) and potassium (K), in that order, and can help you choose a product that suits your needs. I noted above which amendments are helpful in adding nitrogen. Here is a list of just a few products you can use to add phosphorous, potassium or trace minerals:

To Add Phosphorus

Bone Meal: (2-11-0) Made of powdered animal bones, this product is usually added in the early spring and it slowly releases phosphorus into the soil.

Rock Phosphate: (0-3-0) This rock powder slowly releases phosphorus into the soil and some mix it into water and pour it into their planting hole before they plant their tree.

To Add Potassium

Greensand: (0-1-7) This product contains deposits of minerals mined from ancient sea beds. In addition to adding potassium, this product is

Many amendments are made of mined rocks and minerals

rich in other trace minerals. It also improves the texture of soil and helps soil to retain moisture.

Sul-Po-Mag: (0-0-22) Made of mined rock, this product boosts potassium, but it also adds magnesium to your soil and is good to use if your soil is low in magnesium as well.

To Add Trace Minerals

Mineral amendments are made of mined rocks and minerals and sometimes we need to use them to correct soil balance. For instance, if your soil is too acidic, you can apply lime, made of limestone, to make the soil more alkaline. The problem is that you need to add these amendments cautiously. If you add too much, you can seriously damage your soil.

Kelp Meal: This type of granular, dehydrated seaweed has a wide variety of micronutrients as well as boron, copper, iron and manganese.

Azomite®: Extracted from ancient aluminum silicate clay deposits, this product contains more than 50 minerals that are great for plants.

Ask a Local Expert

These are just a few of the amendments available to the organic fruit grower. Always read the instructions on the packaging and apply the product correctly, to avoid damaging your soil. When in doubt, find a local expert (see Resources and Links) to help you interpret your soil test results and to determine appropriate amendments.

Organic Versus Synthetic Fertilizers

This chapter focuses on organic products that you can use to care for your fruit tree. But there are also synthetic fertilizers available at garden centres. Here is the difference:

Synthetic products are man-made. They might be produced through chemical reactions. Synthetic products can be damaging in various ways. Some seep into the groundwater and then wash into rivers and lakes, disrupting the ecological balance. Others give your plants a quick boost but don't feed the living organisms in the soil that are essential for plant health. Many consist of only the three main nutrients (N-P-K) while your plants also need a range of secondary and micronutrients for long-term health.

Organic amendments are usually made up of once-living materials sourced from decomposed plants, insects and animals. These products include animal manures, bloodmeal (powdered animal blood), bonemeal (from finely ground bone) and fishmeal (derived from whole fish) and more. Organic products release their nutrients into the soil slowly over time, feeding the organisms in the soil as well as the plants themselves. When applied correctly, they are non-polluting, but in excess they can also be damaging to the soil and to groundwater.

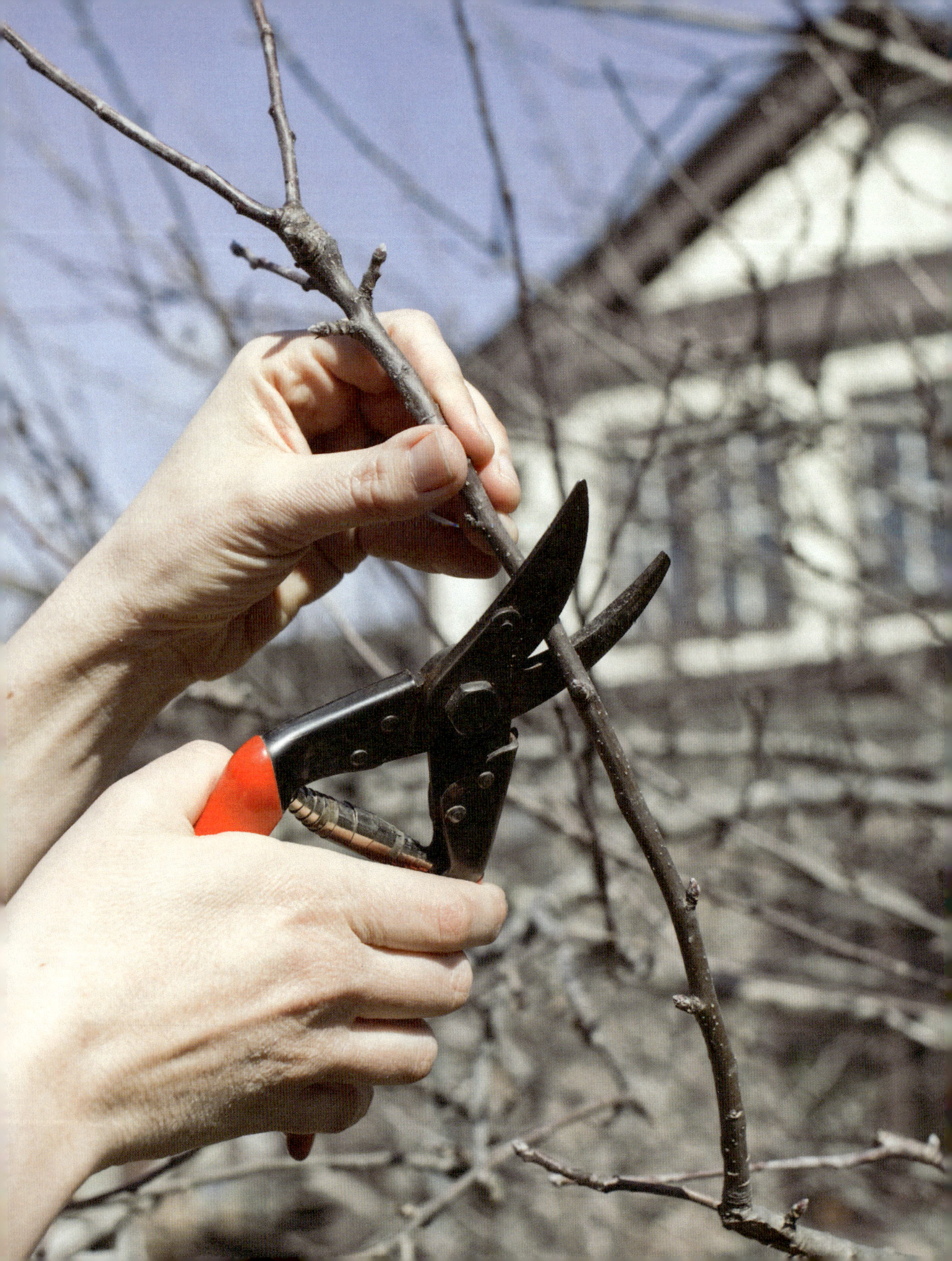

Chapter 8
Pruning Your Trees

The first pruning workshop we held in our park was in 2010. I spent months looking for someone in Toronto who could teach us, but couldn't find a local teacher. So I turned to the experts from the Niagara region – also known as Ontario's "Fruit Belt" – and found Norm Herbert, the former orchard manager for E.D. Smith Farms. He had pruned and cared for thousands of trees during his career.

Norm is a great communicator and a gentle, grandfatherly man, and he was willing to drive more than two hours to come to our park to teach us. On a cold day in March, 25 of us gathered around our orchard harvest table and Norm explained the concepts behind pruning, which allows us to shape our trees so that we can maximize fruit production, trigger tree growth and improve the tree's health. It all made sense.

Then Norm started working on our trees. He had us all gasping in horror as, with a few crazy clips of his hand pruners, he cut some of our trees down to half their size. We had spent months dragging buckets of water around our park to water our trees so they would grow well, and all our hard work vanished with one brutal snip of Norm's pruners! He joked and had a grand old time as he took us through our orchard and methodically hacked away at our trees.

And yet, as Norm explained why he made the cuts he did, we started to understand the theory and practice of pruning. Norm wasn't doing this just to torment us. He was teaching us the importance of being bold when pruning young trees, for their own good and for the good of future harvests. Sure, in the short run our trees looked like they had been butchered. But like all others aspects of gardening, pruning teaches the art of patience. Cutting them boldly (and correctly) in the early spring will result in vigorous growth in the months to come, and will ultimately give you better and stronger trees.

We loved Norm as a teacher, and despite the trauma of that first workshop, we invited him back to teach us in our orchard many times after that. What we learned from Norm and our other teachers is to prune annually. Prune well. And then enjoy stronger, healthier and more productive trees.

Why Do We Prune?

So why do we prune our fruit trees regularly? Here are a few good reasons:

- To ensure each branch has equal access to sunshine, promoting healthy leaves and fruit.
- To allow good air circulation within the tree's canopy, thereby preventing disease.
- To have fewer but more productive branches, allowing you to grow larger, healthier and sweeter fruit.
- To keep your tree to a size that is easier to spray, prune or harvest. Even trees grown on standard rootstock can be pruned to function as smaller trees.
- To train your tree to grow into a sturdy shape that will be strong enough to hold a large amount of fruit.
- To remove non-productive vertical branches (water sprouts) and branches growing at awkward angles that will not produce a good amount of fruit.

When to Prune

When do you prune? Well, that depends on what you want to accomplish.

Winter Pruning

You prune in the late winter/early spring when you want to create your tree's basic structure. The tree is dormant at this time. The buds have not yet swelled and there are no leaves, so it is easy to see each of the branches and to create a form that will work for years to come. You also prune in the winter when you want to stimulate growth in your fruit tree.

Summer Pruning

You prune in the summer when you want to remove diseased or dead branches. This is also the time to prune out branches that are shading large parts of the tree. Because your tree is in full leaf at this time, you can see the shading effects some branches may have. This is a good time to remove water sprouts and suckers. Summer pruning does not stimulate growth as much as winter pruning, so if you want to avoid triggering vigorous growth, this is the time to prune.

Buy good quality tools and keep them clean and sharp, since smooth cuts heal more quickly

When Do You Not Prune?

If possible, you do not prune when it's raining, damp or very humid. These are conditions that diseases love. So to avoid spreading disease, only prune on dry days. That said, those who live in coastal regions, where rain continues throughout the winter, often have little choice. But prune on a dry day if you can.

Pruning Tools

There are four types of tools you will need when you prune your fruit tree. Buy good quality tools and keep them clean and sharp, since smooth cuts heal more quickly.

Hand pruners

Also known as secateurs, these small pruners are operated with one hand and they are useful for clipping young or thin branches. There are many different types of hand pruners available. Try them to see what feels comfortable in your hand.

Limb loppers

This is a long-handled tool that will help you cut through thicker limbs. You will use both hands to cut a limb with a lopper.

Pruning saws

Once your trees are old enough, there may be some branches that are too thick for your loppers. Here your option is to use a pruning saw. They come in many different sizes. A hand pruning saw is small enough to use in tight spaces. If you keep your tree relatively small, then this may be the only saw you will need.

Pole pruners

If you keep your tree relatively small, less than 300 cm (10 feet), then you won't need a pole pruner. But if you have inherited a larger tree, you may want to invest in this tool. Think of it as a limb lopper or hand pruner on stilts. It will help you prune large trees without having to stand on a ladder.

Pruning Approaches

There are a number of approaches to pruning fruit trees, but all of our teachers have promoted the central leader style of pruning. The goal is to create a stable structure for the fruit to grow on, in which all the branches have equal access to sunshine, lots of room for fruit and good air circulation.

In central leader pruning, the goal is to grow a tree that is shaped like a cone or a Christmas tree, with one central branch in the middle. The branches below the central leader become wider and the widest branches are near the bottom of the tree. We use this approach with our apple, pear, plum, apricot and cherry trees.

Definitions for the Parts of the Tree You Will Be Pruning

Central leader
This is the strong, stable branch that will function as the continuation of the trunk of the tree.

Scaffold branches
The scaffold branches are the branches that grow out of the tree's trunk.

Platform
A platform is a set of three to five scaffold branches radiating out from the trunk

Lateral branches
Lateral branches grow off the scaffold branches.

Pruning Cuts
There are two different kinds of pruning cuts you will use on your trees.

Thinning out cuts
A thinning out cut will remove an entire branch from your tree. So if the branch you are removing is a scaffold branch, it will be cut back to the tree's trunk. If the branch is a lateral branch, you will cut back to the scaffold branch (see illustration on page 69).

But how close do you cut to the tree's trunk? The tree will tell you. At the base of every branch there is a thicker area called a collar. The collar contains a substance that will help the tree heal the wound resulting from the cut. So you need to prune your branch back to the collar without pruning off the collar. If you remove the collar, the cut will not heal. And if you don't prune close enough, and leave a stub, the collar also cannot do its work.

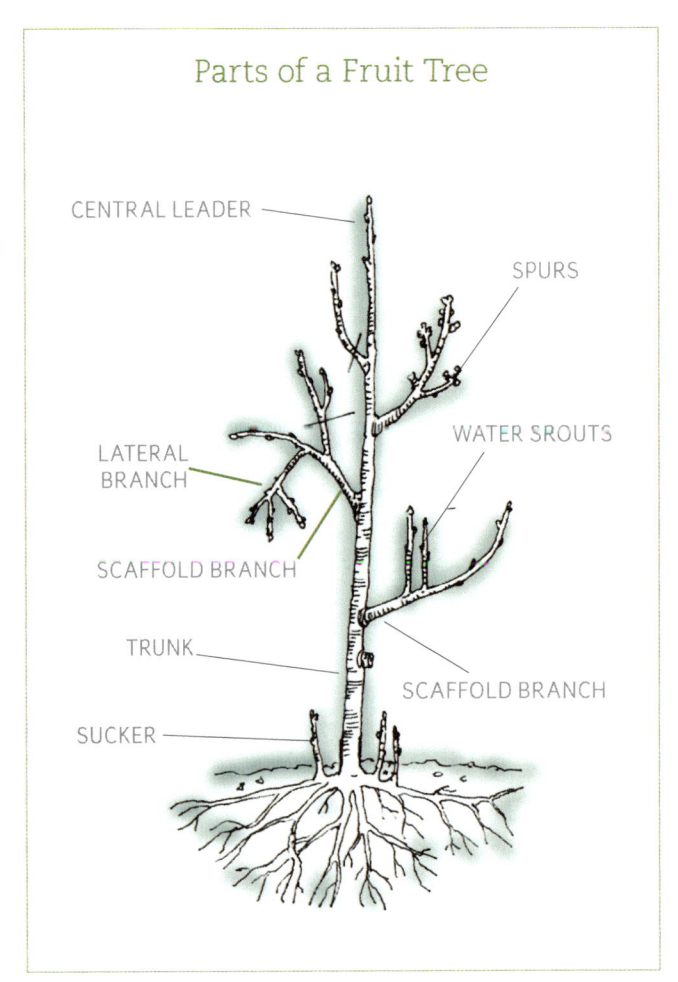

Heading back cuts
These cuts involve shortening a branch. You can head back a branch that is growing too long to be stable, or that is jutting into a neighbouring tree. You can even head your central leader when you don't want your tree to get too tall. The key to heading back cuts is that you must cut the branch just after a bud. Take note of which side of the branch the

Parts of a Fruit Tree

- CENTRAL LEADER
- SPURS
- WATER SROUTS
- LATERAL BRANCH
- SCAFFOLD BRANCH
- TRUNK
- SCAFFOLD BRANCH
- SUCKER

bud is located on. Usually, you will want to choose an outward-facing bud since that bud will grow into a branch. If you choose an outward facing bud, your branch will grow out and away from your trunk. If you choose an inward facing bud, the new branch will grow inward toward the trunk and will likely restrict air circulation in the tree or crisscross with another branch.

So now you know the types of limbs and branches you will be working, the tools you will be using and the type of pruning cuts you will use. You are now ready to prune your trees. And it's easier than you think.

Pruning Young Trees

Your major pruning will take place in the first three years after you plant your tree. After year three, you will simply maintain that structure. As a general rule, you never prune away more than 25 percent of your tree in any given year. See the five steps to winter pruning on pages 70 and 71.

Thinning Out a Scaffold Branch

NORMAL BRANCH   HEAVY BRANCH

A
1.
2.

B
3. THIRD CUT
2. SECOND CUT
1. FIRST CUT

A: When thinning out a branch, make sure you cut right back to the collar (1). If you leave a stub when thinning out the tree will not heal properly (2).

B: If you are thinning out a heavy branch, use a hand saw and do your cut in three steps so as to avoid tearing the bark of the tree when the heavy branch falls.

Summer Pruning

During the summer, a healthy tree will grow vigorously and there is some pruning that you can do then. When you know what you are doing, pruning can be fun and almost addictive. But don't go nuts! If you are pruning during the summer, remove up to 25 percent of the tree only. Pruning more than that will stress the tree and can result in disease and other problems.

Just think: summer is the time when the tree's leaves create energy through photosynthesis that will keep the tree alive in the summer, and some of the energy will be stored to sustain it through the winter as well. If you cut off too many leafy branches, your tree will have trouble creating enough energy to sustain itself. So, think of summer pruning as some small, corrective cuts like these:

- Remove deadwood, diseased or broken branches.
- Remove water sprouts and suckers.
- Remove crisscrossed branches, retaining the

GROWING URBAN ORCHARDS   69

Winter Pruning for the First Three Years

All major structural pruning of your fruit tree should take place in the late winter or early spring when the tree is dormant and before the buds have broken, as this prevents stress to the tree and encourages vigorous growth. Here are the steps for winter pruning in the early, formative years. These steps are relevant for apples, pears, Asian pears, plums and apricot trees. This approach is relevant for whips that already have a basic branching system (you can prune the very same day that you plant your whip) and it's also relevant for potted trees.

STEP ONE
Identify the Central Leader

Stand back and analyze the structure of the tree. Where does the sun hit the tree? Which parts of the tree are shaded? Consider this before you begin pruning, and keep in mind that you want to ensure all branches of the tree have equal access to sun. Now, choose the strongest vertical middle branch to be the central leader of the tree. This may or may not be the tallest option. But it will be a strong, stable and healthy-looking vertical branch that will become the continuation of the trunk. Identify and thin out (remove) any competing central leader branches.

STEP TWO
Choose Your Scaffold Branches

Stand back again and look at the scaffold branches. Starting from the bottom of the tree, thin out (remove) any branches that are below knee height. Now, look for a set of three to five strong, healthy young branches radiating from the trunk in different directions (north, south, east, west, for example). They will be your first platform. Once you have chosen the branches that will make up your first platform, thin out (remove) any excess scaffold branches in that part of the tree. Next, identify the second set of scaffold branches, about 60 to 90 cm (two to three feet) above your first platform. Make sure that the branches in your second platform are not directly above your first platform, because that would shade out the lower platform. So if the branches in your first platform reached out to north, south, east and west, this next set of scaffold branches would reach out to the northwest, southwest, northeast and southeast. Again, thin out any excess scaffold branches in this part of the tree. If your tree is large enough, you may create a third platform. If not, don't worry. Your tree will grow more next year and give you more options. Once you have created your top platform for this year, head back your central leader so that it's just about a foot above the top platform of your tree, to encourage vigorous growth in years to come.

STEP THREE
Clean Up the Messy Stuff

Remove any broken branches, diseased branches, or crisscrossed branches. Remove any branches that are growing in towards the trunk of the tree, as they will prevent healthy air circulation. If your tree has suckers (which grow out of the ground from the roots of your tree) or water sprouts, (shoots that grow vertically off the scaffold and lateral branches and do not produce fruit) remove those as well. Strange downward-facing branches and upward-facing branches can also be removed. But some types of fruit trees, like apricots, have spurs, short little branches that are laden with fruit buds, and they may point in any direction. Spur-laden branches can be shortened, so that they will be strong enough to support the heavy fruit as it grows and ripens.

STEP FOUR
Snip the Tips

As you work with fruit trees, you will learn to differentiate new growth on lateral and scaffold branches. It is softer and more flexible than older branches. After the first year, the branch will develop a more typical "woody" branch look. When you head back a branch, you will rarely remove more than 50 percent of the new growth. But often you will head back less. I suggest you snip off the last two buds on each branch in order to give your tree energy and encourage it to grow. Remember to head back your central leader each year as well. This is one place on the tree where you can cut off more than 50 percent of new growth as a way to keep your tree a nice accessible size.

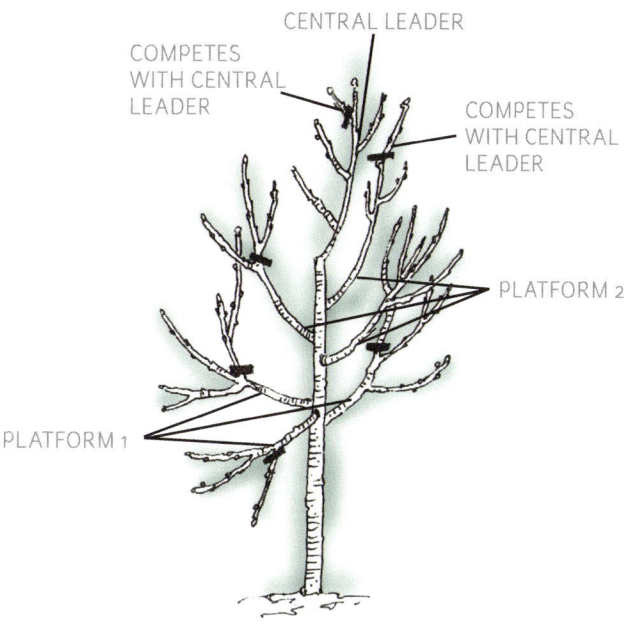

Pruning a Tree
BRANCHES THAT COMPETE WITH THE CENTRAL LEADER SHOULD BE REMOVED, OTHER SUGGESTED CUTS ARE: DOWNWARD BRANCHES, CRISSCROSS BRANCHES, VERTICAL BRANCHES

Most branches will have both leaf bud, which grow tight to the branch and flower buds that are more plump and stick out from the branch.

stronger-looking branch.
- Remove any leafed-out lateral branches that may be blocking sunlight in large parts of your tree.
- Prune out any instances of disease as soon as you find them. More about that later in this chapter and in Chapter 9.

Pruning after the Third Year

By now, you should have a good structure to your tree and you will be allowing your tree to bear fruit. At this point, you can prune your trees in the winter if you want to encourage more vigorous growth, or in the summer if you simply want to maintain the size and health of your tree. After year three, your goals are to:

- Keep your tree about 3 to 3.5 metres (10 to 12 feet) tall. Any taller and it will be difficult to manage. Control the size of your tree by heading back (shortening) the central leader.
- Remove deadwood, diseased or broken branches.
- Remove water sprouts and suckers.
- Remove any branch that might be competing with your central leader.
- Remove branches that are low to the ground.
- To remove crisscrossed branches, retaining the stronger-looking branch.
- Find replacements for any broken or diseased scaffold branches by removing them and allowing newly grown branches to remain and take their place.
- Shorten scaffold branches as necessary in order to keep the conical or Christmas tree shape (with shorter scaffold branches near the top of the tree and longer ones near the bottom).
- Remove any leafed-out lateral branches that may be blocking sunlight in large parts of your tree.

Pruning Out Disease

TOOLS:
- Your pruning tools (hand pruners, loppers, and/or handsaw).
- Bucket containing a mixture of two parts bleach to eight parts water.
- Rag.

1. Ensure it's a dry day. Disease spreads in moist conditions, so never prune your trees on damp or rainy days.

2. Mix up your water and bleach solution in your bucket using 8 parts water to 2 parts bleach.

3. Soak the blades of your tools in the mixture for a minute or two, then wipe them clean with the rag.

4. Once you have identified your problem (oozing clear goop on your branch, or a black dusty buildup, for instance) your goal is to cut it off.

5. Instead of cutting very close to the problem, cut off an extra 6 to 20 cm (two to eight inches) to ensure you are removing infected material hidden inside the branch near the problem area.

6. Place the diseased branch in a garbage bag and dispose of it. Do not put it in the compost as the problem may then spread.

7. After finishing this work, soak the blades of your tools in the bleach solution to disinfect them, wipe them clean with the rag, then move on to the next tree.

Pruning an Established Tree

If you have inherited a tree on your property that has been neglected for many years, it will be harder to create the perfect structure. The tree can be saved, but it will take many years of pruning to get it back into shape. But if the fruit is fantastic and the tree seems healthy, give it a try. Plan to renovate your tree over four years; each year you will prune no more than 25 percent of the branches, keeping the following rules in mind:

- Remove deadwood, and diseased and broken branches first.
- Remove water sprouts and suckers.
- Remove scaffold branches that are shading large parts of the tree.
- Remove limbs that are growing too low to the ground.
- Removed limbs that grow inwards and rub up against other branches.
- Remove and carefully dispose of diseased limbs (in the garbage, not the compost).

As a result of being pruned after many years of neglect, your tree may experience a growth spurt, since its energy can be focused on fewer and healthier branches. Within a few years, your tree may start producing well again.

Pruning Hygiene

One orchardist I spoke to had 10,000 trees in her orchard. She had too many trees for her to prune on her own so she hired some "experts" to do the work. What she found was that as a result of the pruning, her trees experienced more disease problems than before.

In these cases, pruning itself is not to blame, but pruning hygiene. If you work with tools that have been used on diseased trees, you may inadvertently spread that disease. That's why many orchardists disinfect their tools each time they move from one tree to another, by soaking the tools' blades in a mixture of eight parts water to two parts bleach and then wiping them clean with a rag. (See "Pruning Out Disease" on page 73.)

As you are pruning, you may see some problems. Is there clear or black goop oozing out of a branch of your tree? Or a dusty-looking black buildup? These problems could be canker or black knot or other infectious fungal, bacterial or viral diseases. Diseased branches should be removed from the tree as soon as possible, then bagged and sealed up in a garbage bag and disposed of in the regular garbage.

Not sure what the problem is? Take a picture of it and submit it to a fruit-tree care forum (see Chapter 10 for resources) for help identifying the issue. Then, if necessary, cut it out. Always sterilize your tools well after pruning a diseased tree.

Pruning Peaches and Nectarines

Toronto is a little cold to grow peach or nectarine trees, which are susceptible to winter cold and insect damage. And yet, some people do buy them and grow them here with mixed success. In Ben Nobleman Park Community Orchard, our goal is to find and grow the toughest, most disease-resistant types of trees, and peach trees are definitely not on that list.

Peach and nectarine trees are also relatively short-lived. You can wait up to five years for your first harvest, but your tree may only have

A well pruned tree has good air circulation around all the branches.

a lifespan of 10 to 15 years. If you are hoping to grow a tree that will be a legacy for generations to come, this is not the tree to plant.

But some people love these fruits and live in warmer, sheltered regions where they do thrive. If you opt for these trees, you can still use the central leader pruning approach, but keep in mind that peaches and nectarines grow differently than the other types of fruit trees discussed in this book.

While most apple, pear, plum and cherry trees will grow fruit all along the branches, no matter how many years old the branch is, peaches usually only produce fruit on the previous year's growth. That means that if you prune all the new growth off of your peach or nectarine tree, you will not have any fruit at all.

In order to avoid this type of problem, just make sure that each year you head back no more than 25 percent of new growth on your peach and nectarine trees. That's enough to help spur growth in your tree without destroying the fruiting potential for that year.

Orchard Inspiration: Training Orchard Stewards at City Fruit in Seattle

Many municipalities offer allotment gardens, where community members can have access to garden space on public land for a nominal fee. In Seattle, Washington, these gardens are called P-Patches. P-Patches are named after the Picardo family, pioneers from Italy who owned farmland in Wedgewood, an area of Seattle. In the 1960s, the Picardo family leased part of the land to the city to be used as allotment gardens. Later, the city purchased the land outright.

The P-Patch program spread around the city and today there are more than 50 P-Patches in Seattle. But the original Picardo Farm P-Patch still thrives half a century after its establishment, and it is a wonderland of urban gardening creativity. Its 9,000 square metres (98,000 square feet) includes 250 allotment gardens, a delightful jumble of individual vegetable, flower and herb beds, outdoor and indoor classrooms and a water garden. The group even raised money for a composting toilet on site for visiting volunteers. Not long ago, Picardo volunteers decided to plant fruit trees on the site too. But they didn't have all the skills they needed to care for the fruit trees.

That's where a local non-profit group called City Fruit stepped in. They realized that there were many sites around Seattle that had fruit trees and few had volunteers who knew how to care for them. So City Fruit, primarily an urban fruit-harvesting organization, established an "Orchard Steward" program in 2010. They offered volunteers six hours of free training to learn key orchard-keeping skills, and in return the volunteers promised to lead activities in their local orchards for at least two years. The program was a great success and was expanded in 2011. Now City Fruit Orchard Stewards lead groups in 30 P-Patches and other urban orchards around Seattle.

76 GROWING URBAN ORCHARDS

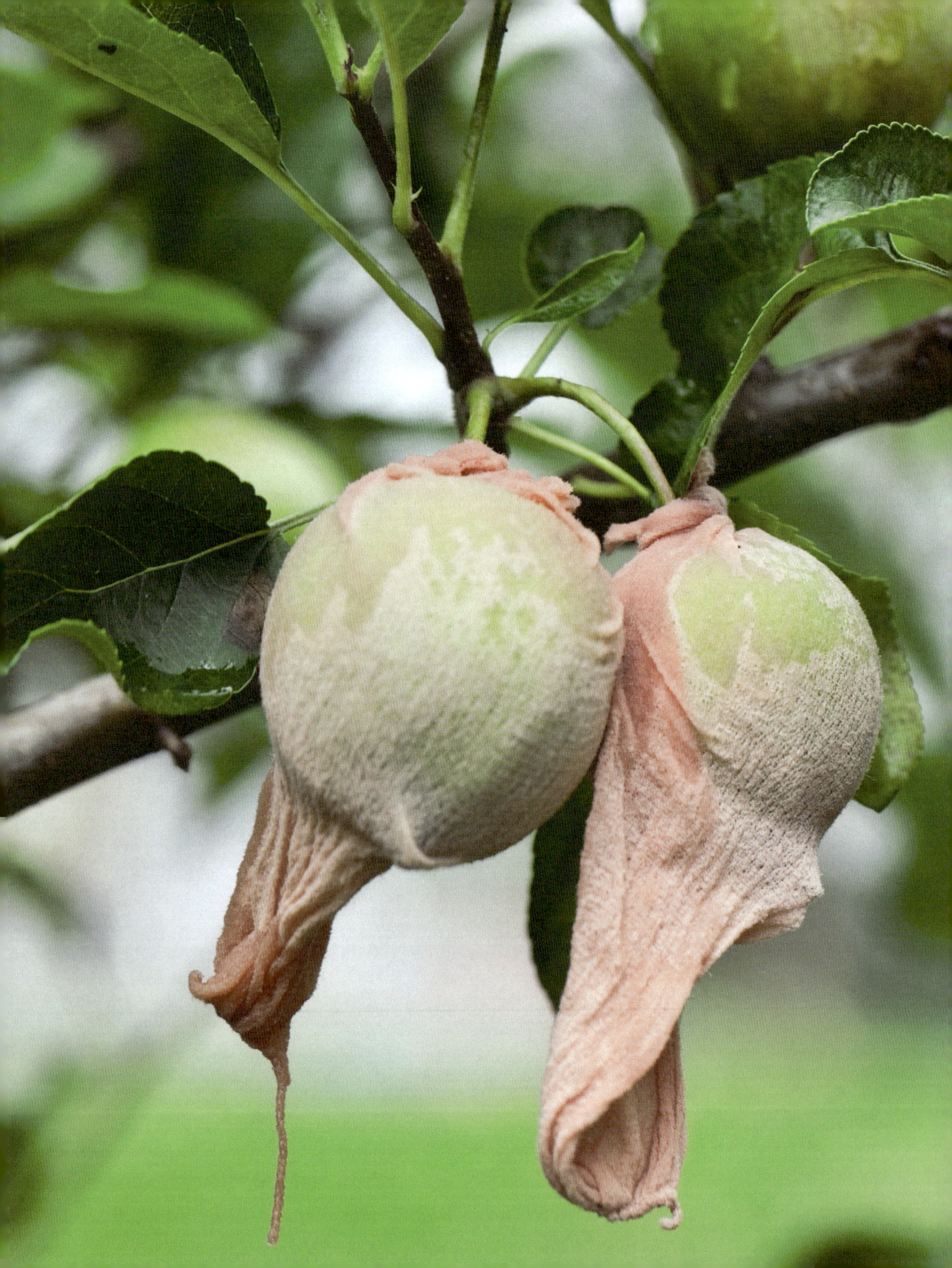

Chapter 9

Preventing Pests and Disease

In Ben Nobleman Park Community Orchard, we encountered our first disease problem early on. We planted our three pear trees in 2009, and that year I noticed that some of the leaves had orange spots on them. I hoped the spots would go away over time. In 2010, I noticed the number of spots had multiplied. It looked like our young trees had chicken pox. I was concerned, but I wasn't sure who to ask for help. So again I hoped our spotty leaf problem would pass.

By 2011 there was no doubt that we had a serious problem. Our trees' leaves – once dark green and shiny – were now grey and covered with orange spots. I finally dared to have a close look at the infected leaves. Underneath the orange spots, on the underside of the leaves, I found an explosion of ugly blisters and bubbles. Our trees had become stunted and weak because those nasty spots prevented the leaves from manufacturing food for the tree.

After a few frantic emails asking for help identifying this problem, I found out that this was pear rust, a fungal disease that has spread like wildfire in our city in the past few years. At this point, our young trees were so badly infected that they had to be removed (we replaced them with disease-resistant apples). And so it was in 2011 that I finally realized that "hoping for the best," as a strategy to protect our trees from pests and disease, just doesn't work.

In previous chapters, you have learned the importance of choosing and planting disease-resistant trees and improving the soil as two important ways to keep your trees healthy. Still, under certain conditions, even strong, disease-resistant trees can suffer from insect infestation or disease. That's why it's essential to learn to recognize and prevent pests and diseases before they become a problem.

For a beginner, learning how to identify the many possible insect and disease problems that they may face in the future can be discouraging and overwhelming. This chapter will show you how to prevent these problems using a multipronged approach, which involves biodiversity, insect control and protective sprays.

For this approach to work, however, you need to monitor your trees regularly and take note of changes early, so that you can identify the problem and correct it before it's too late.

Boosting Biodiversity

It can feel like nature is working against us when we encounter pest and disease problems in our orchards. But actually, these problems are often a sign of an imbalance that nature is trying to correct. A healthy ecosystem has a high level of biodiversity, which means it will have a wide range of plants, animals and insects in it.

And yet, our gardens are rarely shining examples of biodiversity. Instead, many of us have backyard monocultures where grass is the predominant plant growing alongside our fruit trees. To increase biodiversity, you want to include a wider mix of plants in your orchard by integrating other plants like annuals, perennials and shrubs. These plants will bring nutrients to the soil, attract beneficial insects and repel the types of insects we don't want in the orchard. Here are two easy ways to increase biodiversity in your orchard:

Annuals and Perennials

There are certain types of aromatic plants that orchard pests such as spider mites, leafrollers, ants and aphids don't like, including garlic, basil, thyme and lavender. Chives repel Japanese beetles. Flowering plants such as marigold, geraniums and helianthus also help battle bugs such as aphids and whiteflies. Include these plants in a pest control garden bed near your fruit trees. In the very same bed, you can also integrate plants that will attract beneficial insects like pollinators. Great pollinator plants include bee balm, parsley, dill, coriander, echinacea and flowers from the aster family.

Berries and shrubs

Bugs aren't that smart. Confuse them by planting other edibles in your garden, like strawberries, raspberries and blueberries. The added bonus is that doing this will extend your harvest season, as you'll have different types of fruits and berries at different times of the year.

There are lots of beneficial insects that we want in our orchards, like native bees, honeybees, butterflies and other pollinators

Insect Deterrents

There are lots of beneficial insects that we want in our orchards, like native bees, honeybees, butterflies and other pollinators. But fruit trees also attract the types of bugs that can suck the life out of your trees if they lay their eggs inside your tree's bark, or if they feast on the bark or leaves. Insects, of course, also love fruit as much as we do, and can leave your fruit wormy, malformed and inedible. But there are a number of simple and creative ways to prevent or minimize insect problems.

Birdhouses

Every orchard should have a good birdhouse. After all, who would say no to having a family of full-time pest-control workers monitoring their trees and gobbling up the insects that attack them? A nesting family of tree swallows, for instance, will eat an estimated 300,000 insects a year, including beetles, maggots and moths that might otherwise feast on your tree leaves and fruit. Not all birdhouses will work, though. Buy or make a birdhouse that is specially designed for tree swallows or bluebirds, and one that can be cleaned and checked at least once a year in the early spring. If you have lots of trees, make sure you also have a lot of birdhouses.

White Latex Paint

It's easy to recognize the fruit trees in Ben Nobleman Park at any time of year. That's because we've painted the bottoms of our tree trunks with diluted white latex paint from 2.5 cm (one inch) below the soil line to about 24 inches up the trunk. White latex paint (diluted with equal parts of water) is slippery and makes it difficult for crawling bugs like aphids to climb the tree. Finally, whitewashing your tree will help reflect the sun during hot days and protect the tender bark of a young tree from splitting as a result of sun damage. (Older trees have thicker bark and are more resistant to sunburn.) Injured bark is susceptible to attack by wood-boring insects and can result in wood decay.

Collecting Fallen Fruit and Leaves

Cleaning as you go pays off in an orchard environment. Because fruit trees are vulnerable to pests and disease, fallen fruit and fallen leaves can make a wonderful home where pests can curl up, be fruitful and multiply. Rake regularly. Bag up infected fruit and leaves and put them in the garbage so the problem doesn't spread. If the fallen leaves and fruit look healthy, you can put them in the compost.

Tanglefoot Spray

For each fruit tree, spray two red balls (plastic apples, or Styrofoam balls painted red) with Tanglefoot spray. The bugs will be attracted to the red ball, thinking it is a lovely piece of fruit. Then they get stuck in the gluey substance where they will get dehydrated and die. Once the balls are covered with bugs you can pick off the dead bugs and debris and reapply the glue as needed. These traps, available online or at your garden centre, are effective for apple, pear, apricot and plum trees.

Apple Maggot Barriers

These barriers, also called "footies" or "orchard sox," are probably the best way that you can protect the fruit on your apple or pear trees. Wait until the baby fruit on your tree is about the size of a quarter and then slide one of these nylon sleeves on each little fruit, securing them tightly at the base by tying a knot (or you can slip on a 3/8-inch orthodontist rubber band). Your fruit will continue to grow, but the maggots will not be able to slip inside. At harvest time, your fruit will be unblemished. While not practical for large-scale orchards, this is a terrific method if you have just a small number of fruit trees.

Monitoring your trees

Prevention is great. But monitoring your trees is also essential. Visit your trees regularly to look for possible problems so that you can research them as necessary and ask for help.

What Are You Looking For (And Hoping Not to Find)?

- Unusual spots on the leaves.
- Skeletonized leaves or leaves that look like an insect has been nibbling on them.
- White powdery stuff on the leaves.
- Goop oozing out of the branches or trunk. This goop may be clear or black. It may be wet, sticky or dry.
- Small bugs crawling up your tree or settling in on the leaves and branches.
- White or grey cocoons on or under your leaves.
- Curled sticky leaves at the tips of growing branches.

Every organic orchard should have a good birdhouse. After all, who can say no to a free pest control team?

Protective Sprays

Many of us have turned to growing fruit organically because we are against the use of toxic pesticides and fungicides in commercial orchards. So the thought of using any type of spray in your orchard may feel distasteful.

Even organic sprays are not always completely safe. Copper is a good example. Copper is one of the components of Bordeaux spray, an "organic" spray that controls disease in fruit trees. But if inhaled or used improperly, copper can be toxic to humans, other mammals and aquatic life.

And yet there are sprays that organic growers use which are relatively safe and effective at preventing diseases if they are used properly. Because these sprays prevent problems, rather than treating problems that have already spread, the key is to get into a routine early on and make spraying part of your regular tree-care duties.

If you follow the instructions in the pruning chapter of this book you will keep your trees small so you will not need a ladder to spray. That makes the job quick and easy. Here are the tools to buy:

Protective Spray Shopping List

- Lime sulphur and dormant oil (you can buy it as a kit with both products included).
- Garden sulphur.
- Insecticidal soap.
- Two large pressurized hand pump sprayers.
- Chemical-resistant gloves
- Anti-splash goggles.
- Garbage bags.
- A plastic tarp to lay on the grass around the tree you are spraying.

Timing is key if you want to spray safely and effectively

Lime Sulphur and Dormant Oil

Lime sulphur is a mixture of hydrated lime and sulphur. Dormant oil is mineral or vegetable oil that is used to suffocate overwintering insects in your trees. If you use this mixture, which is available in kits that you mix up at home, timing is of the essence. It must be used in the late winter or early spring, before the buds of your trees swell and break. It also must be sprayed on a day when the temperature will remain at or above 0 degrees Celsius (32 degrees Fahrenheit) for at least 24 hours.

So, if you go out to your trees and you can see a little bit of green peeking out from the buds, or if there are any blossoms of leaves on your tree, please do not spray. At this point, it is too late and this mixture can damage the leaves or blossoms of your tree. If your buds are tightly closed and it's a bright clear day but the temperature is below zero, please do not spray. Timing is key if you want to spray safely and effectively.

While getting the timing right can be fiddly, it's worth it. This is a spray that many gardeners use even if they do nothing else to protect their tree from pests and disease. It only needs to be applied once a year and is very effective at preventing insect infestations caused by scale, mites, pear psylla, rust and apple scab.

Procedure

1. **Choose a dry afternoon** in late winter or early spring after the last frost when there is little wind.

2. **Examine your tree's buds** carefully to ensure that they are still tightly closed. If you see any green emerging from the buds, it is too late. Do not continue, as the spray will damage the emerging blossoms and leaves.

3. **With permanent marker**, write on one of your two hand pump sprayers "Dormant Spray Only." Rinse it out to ensure that it's clean inside. Read the instructions and warnings on your sprayer.

4. **Mix the lime sulphur and dormant** oil according to package directions. Seal the pump sprayer according to the directions on the sprayer.

5. **Lay a tarp down** under your tree to protect your grass or any plants under the tree from unnecessary contact with the spray.

6. **Spray the entire surface of the tree**, including the trunk and the branches (including the underside of the branches). Ensure the solution gets into any cracks, crevices or wounds where insects love to hide. Do not spray into the wind. Coat the trees, not yourself, with the spray.

7. Mix up more spray as necessary until all of your trees are coated with the mixture. Allow it to dry and then it will be able to do its work.

8. If you are using a pump or pressure sprayer, carefully release the pressure in your sprayer according to instructions. Don't try to open your sprayer without releasing the pressure, or it may explode.

9. Once this is done, open your sprayer, dispose of the remaining solution (try to use up most of the product on your trees so there is little left to pour onto the ground or down the drain, as it is considered toxic waste) and clean all the components of your sprayer with soap and water. Allow it to dry. And put it away in your fruit tree storage kit for use next year.

A Few Warnings

- This must only be used on dormant trees, before the buds swell and break and before any leaves have come out.

- Spray on a day when you know the temperature will remain at or above 0 degrees Celsius (32 degrees Fahrenheit) for at least 24 hours.

- Apply on a day when there is little wind. Wind makes it hard to direct the spray safely.

- Do not use it on apricot trees or on Empire, Mutsu and Red Delicious apples, as the mixture can destroy their bark.

- Spray in the late afternoon when the sun is not too hot, as the sun's rays can be magnified by the drops of solution and burn the leaves.

- Always wear protective gear during applications, including waterproof gloves, eye protection, long sleeves and long trousers.

- Mix up only as much as you need and use it all on the trees so you do not have to dispose of the excess.

- Once you have used your sprayer for this mixture, do not use it for any other chemicals. Mixing chemicals can be dangerous even if there is just a small amount of residue from a previous application.

- Sulphur is an irritant spray so avoid getting it on your skin and keep it away from children.

- Always read and follow the application instructions on the box.

Sulphur Spray

Sulphur spray also known as "garden sulphur" controls fungi by stopping the germination of fungal spores, which will help prevent rust as well as black spot, powdery mildew and apple scab. But once these diseases have spread widely in your orchard, sulphur isn't strong enough to correct the problem. It is used during the growing season (after your trees have finished blossoming). Apply once or twice a month. Use it more frequently if the weather is hot and humid, as these are perfect conditions for the spread of fungal diseases.

Procedure

1. **Choose a dry time** before an anticipated rain, when there is little wind.

2. **Examine your tree** carefully. Remove by hand any leaves that have strange spots on them and dispose of them in a garbage bag (do not put them in the compost as fungal diseases spread easily). If necessary, use a pair of pruners to remove a diseased branch and dispose of it in the garbage.

3. **With permanent marker**, write on one of your two hand pump sprayers "Sulphur Spray Only" so in the future you don't use it for anything else. Read the instructions and warnings on your sprayer.

4. **Mix the sulphur** according to package directions. Seal the pump sprayer according to the directions on the sprayer.

5. **Spray the entire surface** of the tree, including the trunk and the leaves, focusing on the underside of the leaves where fungus often grows. Spray all tree wounds, cracks and crevices.

6. **Mix up more spray** as necessary (each time you open your sprayer unit, remember to release the pressure) until all of your trees are coated with the mixture.

7. **When you are finished**, release the pressure in your sprayer according to instructions. Wash all the components with soap and water and store your equipment for future use.

A Few Warnings

- Do not use lime sulphur instead of sulphur. Lime sulphur is best applied only when the tree is dormant, as it can damage leaves.

- Never spray blossoms. It's OK to spray fruit; just wash before eating.

- Do not use on apricot trees.

- Sulphur is most effective applied prior to anticipated rain, but it must dry completely before the rain begins. If applied right before rainfall, it will not be effective and will wash right off the leaves. Do not apply sulphur during long spells of hot dry weather, as fungal diseases are less likely to spread in a drought.

- Do not spray into the wind. Spray the trees, not yourself.

- Avoid spraying in the hot sun as the sun's rays, magnified in the droplets of solution, can burn the leaves

- Wear chemical-resistant gloves, eye protection, long sleeves and long trousers. Avoid getting sulphur spray on your skin.

- Keep children away while you do this work.

Insecticidal Soap

At the garden centre, you can pick up insecticidal soap, which is an excellent way to get rid of aphids, scales, spider mites, leafrollers or other soft-bodied pests. Essentially, the soap spray will mummify the bugs by drying them out.

The first step is to identify the pest before you spray your trees, because you want to make sure you are spraying the bad guys, not the good guys. So you can feel free to spray aphids, scale, spider mites and leafrollers. But please do not spray bees, butterflies, ladybugs or other beneficial insects.

You need to be able to see the bugs to spray them. There is no point spraying bugless leaves "just in case," since the spray can also dry up your leaves. You'll need to repeat the treatment every day or two until the bugs are gone. By the way, if you don't have insecticidal soap handy, you might want to try just using a strong stream of water from your hose to wash the bugs away. In many cases, even that simple step will work.

Procedure

1. **Ensure it's a dry day** and not too windy. You don't want rainwater washing off the spray right after you apply it. Spray in the late afternoon when the sun is not too hot to avoid burning the leaves.

2. **Spray** any areas of the tree where you can see aphids, mites or other pests. Do not spray bees, butterflies, ladybugs or other beneficial insects.

3. **Allow your soap spray to dry** and repeat daily until the pest problem is gone.

A Few Warnings

- Apply on a dry day. Rain will wash off the solution before it dries properly.

- Spray in the late afternoon when the sun is not too hot as the sun's rays can be magnified by the drops of solution and burn the leaves.

- Always wear your protective gear while you apply it, including waterproof gloves, eye protection, long sleeves and long trousers. (It's just soap, but protective gear is a good habit to get into.)

A Few Common Fruit Tree Diseases

Black Knot is common in cherry and plum trees and this nasty disease spreads quickly. Early signs include a black or brown swelling on the branches of your trees. It's easy to see during winter pruning when there are no leaves on the branches. To prevent its spread, remove the infected branches as soon as possible, cutting 20 cm (eight inches) or more before the problem appears. Then put the infected branch in a garbage bag and dispose of it in the garbage so it cannot continue to spread. Alternatively, you can dig a deep hole in the ground about 90 cm (three feet) and bury the branch. Black knot will not spread in the soil. If a tree is badly infected, it's important to cut it down and remove it so that it will not spread to other nearby fruit trees.

Rust is a problem that is common on apple or pear trees. It's pretty easy to identify, as you will see orange or reddish orange spots appearing on the leaves of your tree. The spots will grow larger over time and develop a bubbly appearance on the underside of the leaf. Too many of these spots can prevent your fruit tree from producing its own food through photosynthesis and can seriously stress your tree and prevent it from producing tasty fruit. Rust is a serious problem in urban orchards, because the fungus overwinters on juniper bushes, which are common in our city gardens. The best way to prevent this problem is to remove infected juniper bushes near your fruit trees. If you can't do that, you can slow the problem down by spraying your trees regularly with sulphur during the rainy season.

Canker is one of those catch-all terms that describes many problems that fruit trees encounter. For instance, if you see clear jelly-like stuff oozing from your tree's branches or trunk, it's probably canker. If you see glossy black patches on the branches or trunk, they are probably canker too. Canker patches may be sticky or they may be dry. Canker comes in many forms and it can be caused by fungal or bacterial infections. Often canker forms on tree wounds. In any case, the treatment is the same: cut the branch off 7.5 cm (three inches) before the disease appears and dispose of it in a sealed plastic bag in the garbage. The best

> Rust is a problem that is common on apple or pear trees.

way to prevent canker problems is to spray any wounds on your tree regularly with sulphur spray and by watering your tree carefully so that tree wounds will not get wet. In other words, don't water your tree with a sprinkler. Instead, water the roots using one of the techniques described in Chapter 6.

Powdery Mildew is a fungal disease that affects lots of plants, not just fruit trees. On a fruit tree that is infected, it will look like a powder has been poured onto the leaves causing some of them to curl up. Powdery mildew spreads in damp conditions. Prevent the problem by pruning your tree well to ensure that the branches are not cramped together and to allow good air circulation to help the tree dry quickly after it rains. Too much shade on a fruit tree can also result in powdery mildew, so prune nearby trees as necessary to ensure sunlight can reach your tree. Regular applications of sulphur spray can also help.

Apple Scab is another common fungal disease that can infect your tree's leaves, blossoms and fruit. Trees that are badly infected will lose their leaves and the fruit they produce will be inedible. You may see brown or olive green spots on the leaves, which turn dark brown or black over time. Or you may see a small brown scab on your fruit, a scab that slowly grows and becomes deeper brown with a corky or scaly texture. The best way to prevent apple scab is to buy and plant a scab-resistant tree. There are many of them on the market, such as Redfree, Spartan and Liberty apples.

Pear rust on a pear tree in Ben Nobleman Park.

A Few Common Fruit Tree Pests

There are quite a few pests that can seriously damage our fruit trees. Some of them might be familiar to you, as they affect other plants as well. Here are a few common pests that we have found in our orchard:

Japanese beetles are really pretty beetles with a shiny bronze back. But when they flock to your fruit tree you will not like them one bit. They will munch on the leaves of your tree, which will make it hard for your tree to produce the energy it needs through photosynthesis. They also feast on your fruit. Pheromone traps are available, but if you hang one on your tree, it will attract all the neighbourhood Japanese

Orchard Inspiration: Piper's Orchard, Seattle, Washington State

Imagine exploring a huge, sprawling park and stumbling upon a century-old orchard that had long been hidden by an overgrowth of wild blackberry bushes and self-seeded maple trees. That is what happened to landscape architect Daphne Lewis in 1981, when she was working on a survey of Carcreek Park in Seattle, Washington.

The park itself had been established in 1928. It integrated vast amounts of land, including a 1.5-acre plot that the city had purchased from the descendants of a pioneer from Bavaria named Andrew Piper. Piper had been a successful baker in Seattle in the late 1800s. In 1890, he bought this plot of land and planted an orchard.

Piper died in 1904 and his children and grandchildren sold the land to the city. By the time they sold the land to the city, the old fruit trees were already lost in the brush. But when Daphne Lewis discovered that these century-old fruit trees had survived, she was determined to save them, and she inspired the local community to get involved.

It took more than two years for volunteers from the local community, working together with Seattle's Parks Department and member of the Seattle Fruit Tree Society, to clear the land around the trees. They discovered that 29 of the original heirloom orchard trees had survived. Over the last three decades, they have cared for and harvested the trees and planted more young trees as well.

Piper's Orchard faces the challenges that all other orchards face like pests and disease. According to Bob Baines, Park Maintenance Crew Chief, Seattle Parks and Recreation, their biggest decision was about pesticide use.

"It's a public park. It's not a commercial orchard. So the apples have no financial value. If there is no crop, then it's not a big problem so we do not spray to preserve the crop.

Piper's orchard had a problem with apple maggots for many years and the real concern was not the lost fruit but the possibility that the pests would spread to nearby commercial fruit growing areas.

"Our solution was to get all the volunteers to clean up and dispose of the fallen fruit. Now we have yard waste bins that get collected once a week. As a result we have less of a problem with pests."

Today, Piper's Orchard's volunteers are proud to keep the legacy of the Piper family alive by caring for those beautiful, century-old trees. Each year they celebrate that history with the annual Festival of Fruit, where all are welcome to come and enjoy music, a pie-judging contest, a cider press demonstration and educational orchard tours.

Some of the apple trees in Piper's Orchard are over one hundred years old.

beetles to your tree, making your problem worse (some will get caught in your trap). Our approach is to go out into the orchard with a bowl of water with a squirt of dishwashing liquid and a splash of rubbing alcohol in it. We use a twig or leaf to sweep the beetles off the leaves and into the water. Japanese beetles can't swim, so they quickly drown.

Aphids are also familiar to anyone who has grown a vegetable or flower garden. They are little pear shaped insects that suck the sap out of your plants and trees. One of the best ways to deal with these little guys is to wash them off your tree with a strong stream of water. I've found spraying them with commercial insecticidal soap also helps. But most importantly, remember to spray your trees with lime sulphur and dormant oil in the early spring, as this will kill overwintering aphid eggs and prevent a problem in the season to come.

Cocoons, are very common, and never good news. I have seen them on many trees and what I have learned is that when you see them, remove and destroy them right away. Stomping on cocoons may seem cruel, but the critters that will soon emerge from that cocoon will be fruitful, multiply and seriously damage your tree. They may be tent caterpillars, by the way.

In which case, you don't even need to stomp on the caterpillars inside. Just use a stick and hit the cocoon until it opens and allow the birds to enjoy a caterpillar buffet.

Learn to identify these by researching them online. Hopefully, you will never find them on your orchard trees ... but most likely you will at some point in time.

Researching Pests and Disease in Your Region

What are the problems that fruit growers face near you? They won't necessarily be the same ones that we face in Ben Nobleman Park Community Orchard. For instance, here, we have a real problem with black knot, but that fungal disease is rarely a problem in Saskatchewan or Alberta.

So how do you research fruit tree pests and diseases that are common in your region? In the United States, there are county extension offices that are centres for research in subjects including agriculture and pest management. They have lots of information online and staff members are available to answer your questions about gardening, agriculture and pest control. In Canada, it's best to turn to your province's department of agriculture, which will have excellent regional resources and a help line.

And wherever you are, if you are lucky enough to have a local nursery that specializes in fruit trees, it's a good idea to consult with them. If you are going to bring in a diseased clipping or leaf from your tree, however, do make sure it's sealed into a plastic bag so that the disease doesn't spread to their trees.

The Holistic Approach

If you're sick, you can go to the doctor and he may prescribe some medicine to heal you. That medicine may have side effects. It may work and it may not. Or you might consider a holistic approach: ensure you eat a highly nutritious diet, get lots of exercise and fresh air, learn to meditate or do yoga to combat stress.

There are a growing number of orchardists who are taking this approach with their fruit trees. Instead of spraying their trees with organic sprays that prevent disease, they spray their trees with nutrient-rich products that enhance tree health. A healthy tree is less likely to succumb to problems like disease and insect infestation.

One of the pioneers promoting this approach is Michael Phillips, the author of "The Apple Grower" and "The Holistic Orchard." Instead of spraying with sulphur and other fungicidal products, his sprays are applied in rhythm with tree root growing cycles and include ingredients such as liquid fish fertilizer (not fish emulsion, which has been pasteurized), pure neem oil, nettle tea, comfrey tea, effective microbes and molasses.

One key tool he uses is a product called Surround Kaolin Clay Spray, which is mostly made up of a clay mineral. The latter must be applied soon after petal fall, when the fruit is still very small. Unfortunately, in many municipalities, Surround is not available to home growers and can only be applied by an expert with a pesticide licence.

Michael Phillips' approach is very exciting and has great potential. It is a little complicated for a novice grower, however. Still, it's definitely worth reading his wonderful book.

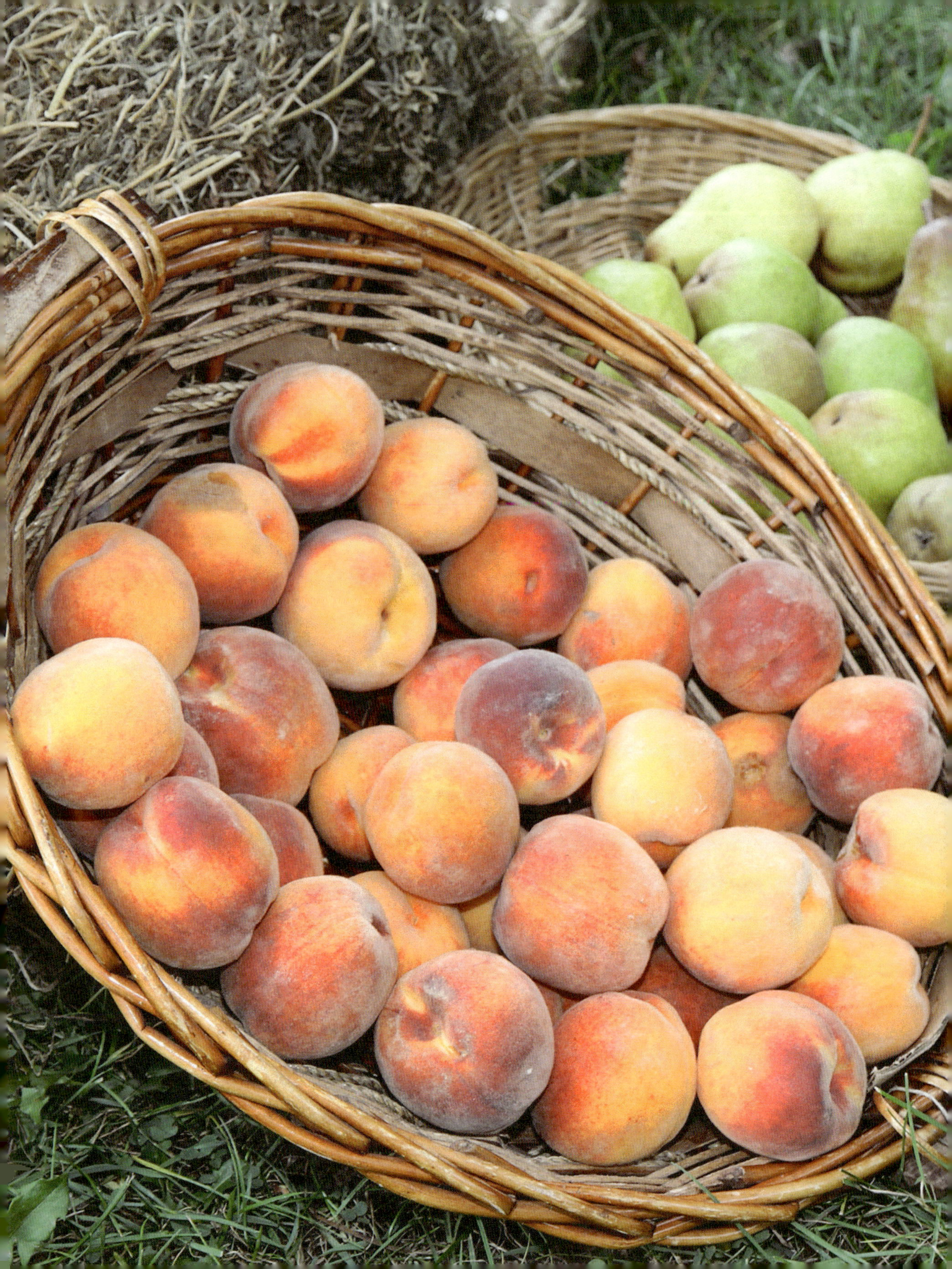

Chapter 10
Anticipating the Harvest

The first three years that our fruit trees were in the ground, our goal was to help them establish themselves. So each spring, after pollination, we carefully plucked the baby fruit off each and every tree. It was good for the trees, allowing them to focus their limited energy on expanding their root systems. But for us, it was a heart-wrenching process. Without baby fruit, we had no hopes of having a harvest that year. And yet, a well-established tree will be healthier and produce better harvests in the long term. So we did what we had to do.

By 2012, our trees were strong and established enough to support a harvest. We were so excited to taste the fruit! Sadly, that was not to be. The weather that year was erratic, with an early spring punctuated by harsh frosts. Our trees, like many others in the region, were not successfully pollinated and did not set fruit. We sighed and moved on, knowing that we would have to wait yet another year to taste our harvest.

The spring of 2013 was so much better, with lots of rain and stable temperatures. Our trees blossomed beautifully and the pollinators did their work. Soon, baby cherries, apricots and apples appeared on our trees and we watched with pleasure as they grew. In July the cherries,

Dreaming of a cherry harvest in years to come.

were just about ready to pick. Our plan was to harvest and share the bounty on a mid-month stewardship day.

Then, just two days before our planned harvest, something strange happened. My colleague Lynn Nicholas and I were giving a visitor a tour of our park when we noticed that our cherry trees, previously laden with ripe fruit, were fruitless. Every single ripe cherry was gone and all that was left was one lonely cluster of green cherries. We were in shock. Could the birds or raccoons have taken them? If so, wouldn't they leave behind the pits?

While Lynn and I were trying to figure out what happened, a woman crossing through the park, came up to the cherry tree. She found the remaining cluster of unripe cherries and plucked it off the tree. To me, the situation was becoming more and more surreal.

"Those cherries aren't ripe. Why did you pick them?" I asked, wondering to myself if this was some sort of bad dream.

"Well, I saw a lady yesterday come and fill two bags with cherries and I thought I should pick some before they were all gone," she answered.

"But those cherries aren't ripe," I said, frustrated. "They won't taste good."

"Oh well," she said, and she tossed the cherries on the ground and walked away. I looked at the discarded cherries and my heart sank. That was the last of our cherry harvest for 2013. Now, we would have to wait another year – 12 more long months – until we would have an opportunity to taste them again.

I know that when you plant fruit trees in a public park, there really is no guarantee that you will ever be able to enjoy the harvest yourself. And the point of our orchard is to feed our community. But knowing one person was hogging the harvest really got my goat. So I was determined to find a way to taste something from our orchard that year. The apricots would ripen next.

So each day, I visited the trees, and lingered in the park a little longer than usual. I sat at the harvest table or relaxed on a bench, always keeping my eyes open for suspicious looking loiterers around the fruit-laden trees. As harvest time approached, I picked and crunched on a few not-quite-ripe apricots and they were delicious. For me, eating unripe apricots was an insurance policy: even if someone stripped the trees of fruit in the middle of the night, I would have had a taste before they ran off with the bounty.

Luckily, the cherry bandit did not return and there were plenty of apricots left on those trees for our volunteers, as well as for peckish passersby. We ate them fresh, or grilled them with maple syrup. For people who have spent years waiting for their first harvest, nothing has ever tasted so good.

One day our trees will produce enough fruit to feed all of us — park volunteers, visitors, and even local wildlife. It can take up to 10 years before fruit trees are established enough to give us a full harvest. When you are waiting for your first harvest it may feel like a long time to wait, but it's really the blink of an eye if you consider that fruit trees can live and produce harvests for 15, 25 or even 100 years, depending on the variety and how well they are cared for.

So what will you do when your trees are ready to harvest? A mature fruit tree can produce more than 100 pounds of fruit per year — enough to share with family, friends and neighbours. You can eat it fresh, preserve it for the winter or bake it into pies. I've heard stories of family events where the parents, children and grandchildren gather to harvest their apple trees, taking turns pressing the fruit into cider. Others leave baskets of fruit on their neighbours' doorsteps. Some share excess with the hungry by participating in programs that support those in need, like Plant a Row, Grow a Row.

While sharing is an important part of growing fruit, so is celebration. Some orchards have blossom festivals in the early spring. Across the United Kingdom, orchards celebrate Apple Day in October. In Ben Nobleman Park, we held our first harvest festival in 2010, not long after our first trees were planted. We organized orchard tours, educational booths and music, and we gave out fruit purchased from local farms. The event attracted 400 people from across the city to our little park. I'm not sure our park had ever had that many people in it before.

May your trees give you many opportunities to celebrate. And may your fruit-growing adventure be a rewarding experience. When you first plant your fruit trees, they will look like tiny rooted branches planted in the ground. But as the years go on, they will feel more like friends. You will learn about their likes and dislikes by their reactions to pruning or to the different types of mulch or fertilizers that you apply. The most important thing I have learned from our trees is that every living thing deserves our love, gratitude, care and respect. Enjoy the journey!

Orchard Inspiration: Not Far From The Tree

Wouldn't you love to have a garden that provides you with fruit throughout the growing season? Imagine harvesting serviceberries and mulberries in the spring, cherries, plums and apricots in the summer, and apples and pears in the fall. This is a reality for the 1,000-plus volunteers of Not Far From The Tree. For them, the entire city of Toronto is their garden, and each year they harvest enough fruit to eat fresh, cook with, preserve, freeze and share.

Until 2008, a large share of the estimated 1.5 million pounds of the urban fruit that grows each year in the City of Toronto went to waste because homeowners with productive fruit trees didn't have the time or resources to harvest them. So environmental studies graduate Laura Reinsborough founded Not Far From The Tree. Her goal was to link up homeowners with volunteers who could harvest their trees for them. The resulting bounty would then be divided up with one third going to homeowners, one third going to the volunteers, and one third going to local agencies like the food bank.

Since then, the growing season has become a moveable feast for Not Far From The Tree, which currently harvests up to 22,000 pounds of fruit from urban trees each year. The group has also become known for their events and harvest celebrations. They have organized cider and blossom festivals. They have held canning and preserving workshops. They have even organized "Syrup in the City," a festival to celebrate maple syrup that has been produced from local trees.

In the process, Not Far From The Tree has educated thousands of people about the importance of growing and consuming local fruit and the group's volunteers are helping to build a sustainable local food system.But Not Far From The Tree has also created opportunities for Torontonians to build community as they gather to enjoy the bounty that our urban fruit trees provide.

"Making those connections is what Not Far From The Tree is all about," says Interim Project Director Danielle Goldfinger. "Using our fruit trees – this amazing resource that we have – as a mechanism to bring people together and build community. When it happens, it's an exciting thing."

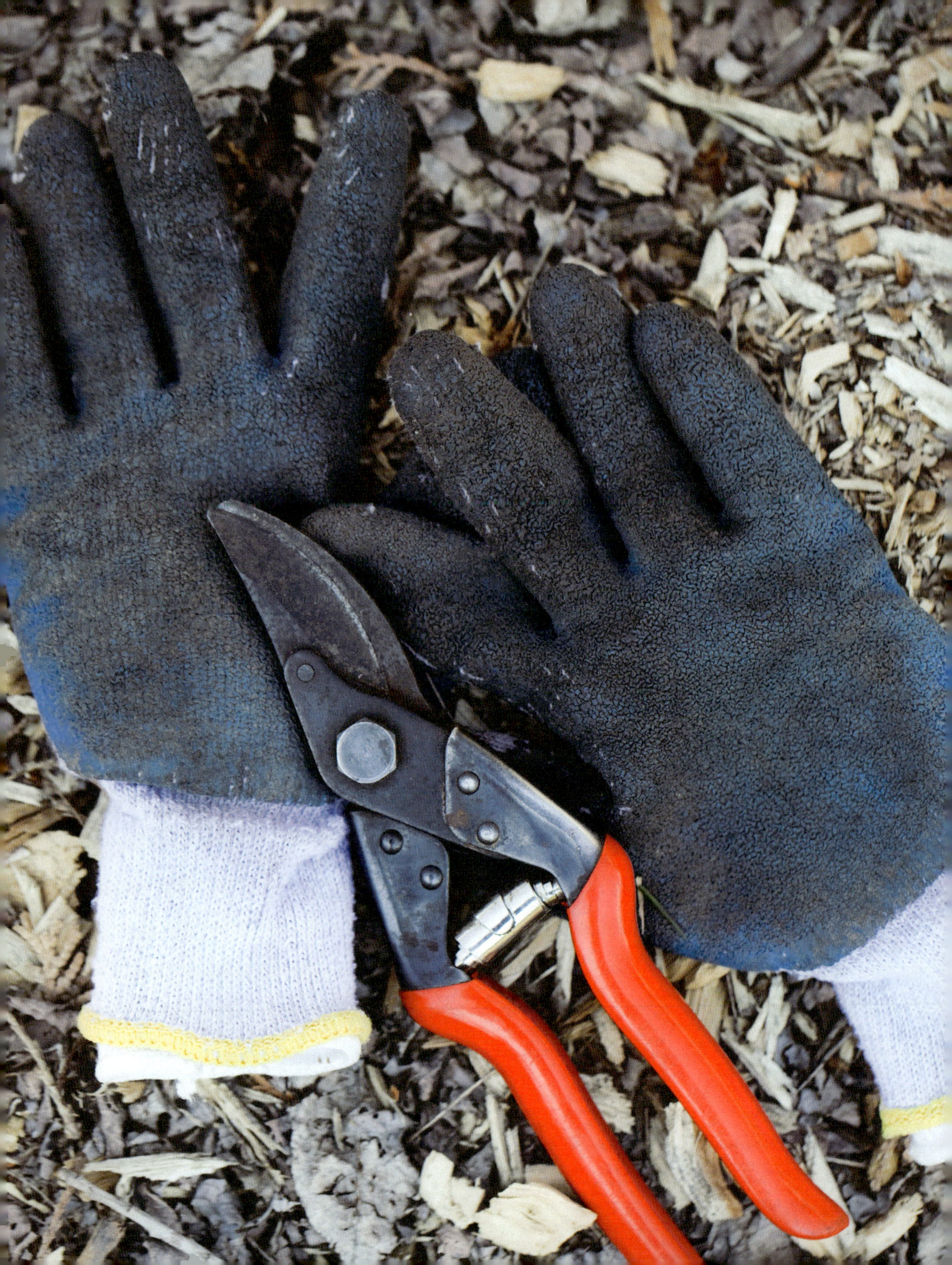

Resources and Links

Are you trying to identify a problem with your fruit tree? Looking for information about a variety and how it's growing for others? Would you like to link up with other people who are passionate about fruit trees so that you can learn from them? On these pages you can see just a few of the top resources online and in person around North America and the United Kingdom. While I cannot recommend any one company or organization in this list, I have found many of their websites useful. Please see this list as a great place to start your own research.

Fruit Tree Care Education

The following organizations are sources of reliable information ranging from how-to articles to online forums where you can link up with other organic fruit growers. Many also do in-person workshops, consulting and more. You may also want to search online for a local university that has a department of agricultural or horticultural studies, as they may have great resources as well.

CANADA

Orchard People
Toronto, Ontario
www.urbanfruittree.com
A company that specializes in fruit tree care and education.
ONLINE: E-learning workshops, school curriculum, books, CDs, links and fruit tree related products and services.
IN PERSON: Orchard consulting, workshops, presentations, and hands-on fruit tree maintenance.

Growing for Green
Toronto, Ontario
www.communityorchard.ca
This voluntary group founded Toronto's first community orchard in a public park.
ONLINE: Information about how to start a community orchard, blog, events listings, educational resources.
IN PERSON: Fruit tree care workshops, harvest festivals, volunteer stewardship, community events and more.

Sharing Farm
Richmond, B.C.
www.sharingfarm.ca
A charity that grows and donates food to local agencies and offers orchard training programs.
ONLINE: Social media, events, blog.
IN PERSON: Fruit Tree Care workshops, university level training in sustainable farming, corporate volunteering and stewardship.

Calgary Community Orchard Pilot Project (Calgary, Alberta)
www.calgary.ca
The City of Calgary is researching different models for growing fruit in the city, including creating and maintaining both city-run orchards and community-run orchards.
ONLINE: A list of orchards in the city and frequently asked questions.
IN PERSON: Support of community groups that plant fruit trees.

Tree Canada
www.treecanada.ca
This charity provides Canadians with education and resources helping them to plant and care for urban and rural trees, and they have recently introduced an "Edible Tree" grant to support groups who want to start school and community orchards across Canada.

UNITED STATES

Seattle Fruit Tree Society (Seattle, Washington)
www.seattletreefruitsociety.com
A fruit tree society supporting home growers.
ONLINE: Resources on fruit tree care, grafting and budding, online heirloom apple ID program.
IN PERSON: Talks, workshops, social events, field trips and more.

Home Orchard Society (Tigard, Oregon)
www.homeorchardsociety.org
A non-profit educational organization for home growers with all levels of experience.
ONLINE: E-books with listings of disease-resistant apple varieties, rootstocks and more, articles on fruit growing, forums where you can find expert advice, quarterly newsletter.
IN PERSON: Orchard tours, festivals, rootstock sales.

City Fruit (Seattle, Washington)
www.cityfruit.org
Fruit harvesting organization in Seattle.
ONLINE: Listings for workshops, events, downloadable PDFs about growing fruit locally.
IN PERSON: Volunteering, fruit harvesting, orchard stewards training program.

Midwest Fruit Explorers (Chicago, Illinois)
www.midfex.org
This non-profit organization links amateur fruit growing enthusiasts around Chicago.
IN PERSON: They hold pruning workshops, festivals and other events.
ONLINE: They have a Q&A page and an inspiring online tour of "Gene's Backyard Orchard".

North American Fruit Explorers
www.nafex.org
A membership-based organization that produces a volunteer-written quarterly journal on growing fruit.
ONLINE: Fruit tree care videos, special interest groups, access to experts on all fruit types.
IN-PERSON: They have an annual conference with hands-on instruction on propagation and care of fruiting trees.

Boston Natural Areas Network
(Boston, Massachusetts)
http://www.bostonnatural.org/outdoorclassroom.htm
This non-profit group took over for Earthworks Boston, a group that planted orchards around the city for more than 20 years.
ONLINE: Free outdoor classroom curriculum materials.
IN PERSON: Volunteering, workshops and events.

Organic Tree Fruit Association
(Madison, Wisconsin)
http://organictreefruit.org
A non-profit membership organization for fruit tree growers.
ONLINE: Research updates on fruit trees from various universities, educational resources, quarterly newsletter for members.
IN PERSON: Day-long seminars, field days and events.

Lawrence Fruit Tree Project
(Lawrence, Kansas)
www.lawrencefruittreeproject.wordpress.com
Promotes access to healthy food by encouraging the public to grow, steward and utilize perennial food plants.
ONLINE: Instructional PDFs, contact lists and resources, including pest and disease factsheets.
IN PERSON: Stewardship, events and workshops.

Portland Fruit Tree Project
(Portland, Oregon)
www.portlandfruit.org
This non-profit group harvests fruit trees across the city and distributes the produce to food banks. They also manage two community orchards on public lands.
ONLINE: They have downloadable PDF guides for beginners about caring for various types of fruit and nut trees.
IN PERSON: They hold workshops on tree care skills and food preservation and have tree care teams who are trained to care for fruit trees in their area.

Fallen Fruit
(Los Angeles, California)
http://fallenfruit.org
This group is has a long list of fruit-based projects including fruit tree mapping on public property, the distribution and planting of bare root trees, communal jam making and more. They started off as an artists' collaboration and their goal is to bring social issues to the fore using photography, video and performance art.

Fruit Tree Planting Foundation
(Pittsburgh, Pennsylvania)
www.ftpf.org
This non-profit charity helps fund and plant orchards around the world and encourages people to grow their fruit trees organically.
IN PERSON: They have grant programs to plant school and community orchards in the United States and around the world.
ONLINE: They have arboricultural resources including quick guides and videos about planting and caring for fruit trees.

International Fruit Tree Association
www.ifruittree.org
This membership-based organization focuses on research and education around dwarf fruit trees and intensive orchard systems.
IN PERSON: They hold an annual educational conference and fruit tree study tours for fruit tree professionals. They also produce a publication called Compact Fruit Tree three times a year.

UNITED KINGDOM

These United Kingdom-based sites offer rich resources that are useful in North America as well.

Orange Pippin
United Kingdom
www.orangepippin.com
ONLINE: Comprehensive resource for apples with information on over more than 600 varieties and listings for 2,000 apple orchards. Forums moderated by experts where you can submit questions about fruit tree care.

Common Ground
United Kingdom
www.commonground.org.uk
ONLINE: A U.K.-based charity that produces books and other materials including *The Community Orchard Handbook* and *The Apple Source Book*.

London Orchard Project
London, England
www.thelondonorchardproject.org
A registered charity works with Londoners to plant and harvest apple, pear and plum trees.

ONLINE: Links to educational resources from Natural England on caring for orchards sustainably.
IN PERSON: Planting community orchards, harvesting projects, revitalizing neglected older orchards, stewardship, volunteering, training and events.

Government Agricultural Resources

If you're looking for information that relates to your region, check out the ministry of agriculture, food and rural affairs in your province or, in the United States, visit your state cooperative extension service office, as they will have factsheets and information specific to your region. They may also be able to recommend experts to help you with fruit tree care.

Master Gardeners

You can also direct your questions to your local master gardener group. Master gardeners receive about 40 hours of training and need to do community service to keep their qualifications up to date. These volunteers can help in a variety of ways, from answering questions online to telephone horticulture care hotlines. Or they will teach workshops to local community groups. Search online for a master gardener group near you and ask to speak to an expert with experience in fruit tree care.

Fruit Tree Suppliers

If you are lucky, you may live near one of the increasing number of innovative garden centres that are stocking disease-resistant fruit trees like Liberty, Redfree and Freedom apples. But if your local garden centre doesn't carry the types of trees that you need, search online for a specialist fruit tree nursery (search "disease resistant fruit trees" and your province or state). Most have online catalogues where you can research your tree as described in Chapter 4. Try to order a tree from a specialist nursery near you, as they will know what thrives in your region. But if you can't find what you want, you can order from further afield, since bare root trees are shipped by post. It may not be possible, however, to ship a tree across the U.S./Canada border. For an updated list of specialist nurseries visit www.urbanfruittree.com.

Soil Testing

There are many soil testing labs across North America, and often it's best to search online and find a testing lab near you. Be sure to ask the lab to interpret the results for you and to specify that you are growing fruit trees, since they have different soil needs than turf, perennials or even vegetables.

One problem you may encounter is that soil test results can be highly technical and difficult to understand. They will tell you how much of each essential nutrient you may need but they will not suggest easy-to-source environmentally friendly products that you can use to amend your soil and how much to add. (Too much of any given nutrient can damage your soil.).

For assistance in interpreting your soil test, visit **www.urbanfruittree.com** and download our e-book "How to read a soil test".

Orchard Inspiration

A number of fantastic organizations and groups were featured in this book. Want to see what they are up to? Check them out on the internet at the web addresses below:

Walnut Way Conservation Corp.
Milwaukee, WI
www.walnutway.org

City of Calgary Community Orchard Research Project
Calgary, Alberta
www.calgary.ca

Sharing Farm Society
Richmond, B.C.
www.sharingfarm.ca

Strathcona Community Garden
Vancouver, B.C.
www.strathconagardens.ca

City Fruit
Seattle, WA
cityfruit.org

Piper's Orchard
Seattle, WA
www.pipersorchard.org

Not Far From The Tree
Toronto, Ontario
www.notfarfromthetree.org

Image Credits
Page numbers highlighted in blue

Illustrations:
9, Map of Ben Nobleman Park Community Orchard, Marlena Zuber
All other illustrations by Sherry Firing

Photographs:
Cover Hand Pruner Holster, Jacklyn Atlas
Cover Blossoming Fruit Tree, Roberto Ricciuti/istockphoto
Cover Apples, Sofia World/istockphoto
Title Page Blossoms, Jacklyn Atlas
Table of Contents Dr. Jose Rizal Park Orchard Seattle, Barbara Erwine/City Fruit
3 Caught Purple Handed, Danny Floh Back, Not Far From The Tree
5 Ben Nobleman Park Volunteers Harvest Festival 2010, Margaret Irving Portraits
6 Picardo Farm, Seattle, Susan Poizner
12 Blossoms, Jacklyn Atlas
23 McIntosh Apples, Ned Jennison/Thinkstock
24 Fruit Tree Label, Susan Poizner
27 Serviceberries, Susan Poizner
28 Apples and Pears for Preserving, Not Far From The Tree
32 Fruit Tree Expert Norm Herbert and a Bare Root Tree, Susan Poizner
34 Strathcona Community Garden Member Edging a Fruit Tree, Susan Poizner
40 Watering Cans on Toronto Island, Alisonh29/Dreamstime
48 Soil Probe, Jacklyn Atlas
50 Susan Poizner Adding Compost, Cliff Changoor
53 Espalier Fruit Trees, Strathcona Community Garden, Susan Poizner
54 Alfalfa mulch, Ben Nobleman Park, Susan Poizner
64 Pruning a Fruit Tree, Jacklyn Atlas
72 Fruit and Leaf Bud Branch, Jacklyn Atlas
73 Pruning Tools, Susan Poizner
75 Well Pruned Apple Tree, Susan Poizner
76 Seattle Community Orchard, Susan Poizner
78 Orchard Sox Protecting Apples, Jacklyn Atlas
82 Orchard Birdhouse, Susan Poizner
89 Pear Rust, Susan Poizner
91 Piper's Orchard in Seattle, Susan Poizner
94 Peaches and Pears, Margaret Irving
96 Local Cherries, Danielle Rosenthal, Not Far From The Tree
100 Gloves and Hand Pruners, Jacklyn Atlas

Bibliography

Carlson, Robert F.
North American Apples: Varieties, Rootstocks Outlook. Michigan State University Press. 1970.

Dolan, Susan.
Fruitful Legacy: A Historic Context of Orchards in the United States. National Park Service. U.S. Department of the Interior. 2009.

Ellis, Barbara W. and Marshall Bradley, Fern.
The Organic Gardener's Handbook of Natural Insect and Disease Control, Rodale Press. 1996.

Gillman, Jeff.
The Truth About Organic Gardening: Benefits, Drawbacks and the Bottom Line. Timber Press. 2008.

Gershuny, Grace.
Start with the Soil: The Organic Gardener's Guide to Improving Soil for Higher Yields, More Beautiful Flowers, and a Healthy, Easy-Care Garden. Rodale Press. 1993.

Hill, Lewis and Perry, Leonard,
The Fruit Gardener's Bible: A Complete Guide to Growing Fruits and Nuts in the Home Garden. Storey Publishing. 2011.

Martin, Carol.
The Apple: A History of Canada's Perfect Fruit. McArthur and Company. 2007.

McMorland Hunter, Jane and Kelly, Chris.
For the Love of an Orchard: Everybody's Guide to Growing & Cooking Orchard Fruit. Pavilion. 2010.

Otto, Stella.
The Backyard Orchardist: A Complete Guide to Growing Fruit Trees in the Home Garden. OttoGraphics. 1993.

Phillips, Michael.
The Apple Grower: A Guide for the Organic Orchardist. Chelsea Green. 2005.

Phillips, Michael.
The Holistic Orchard: Tree Fruits and Berries the Biological Way. Chelsea Green. 2011.

Reich, Lee.
Landscaping with Fruit: Strawberry Ground Covers, Blueberry Hedges, Grape Arbours and 39 Other Luscious Fruits to Make Your Yard an Edible Paradise. Storey Publishing. 2009.

Community Orchard Handbook. Common Ground. 2008.

Rodale Organic Gardening Basics: Soil. Rodale Inc. 2000.

Glossary

Anthers – Male organs of the flowers, which bear pollen.

Bare root tree – A tree that has had all of the soil removed from around its roots in preparation for transplanting.

Bud – A tough, protective sheath that holds inside it everything the tree needs to produce a new leaf or a blossom.

Cambium – The layer of cells underneath the phloem, where new growth occurs.

Central leader – The strong vertical middle branch of a fruit tree.

Chlorophyll – A green pigment in the leaf that absorbs light energy from the sun.

Dormant tree – A tree that is alive, but not actively growing.

Feather – A two-year-old branched fruit tree.

Feeder roots – Tiny roots that emerge from the woody roots of a tree. They grow outwards and upwards and absorb minerals, water and oxygen from the upper surface of the soil.

Fertilization – The process by which the male and female genetic materials of a plant unite.

Fruitwood or scion – A young branch clipped from a tree with desirable fruit, which can be grafted onto rootstock as a way of propagating the tree.

Graft union – The location on the trunk where the rootstock and the fruitwood have been joined together.

Grafting – The practice of fusing two trees together so they will function as a single tree.

Green manure – A crop grown and then tilled into the soil as a way to improve soil quality.

Hardiness – The extent to which a tree is able to withstand cold winter temperatures without protection.

Heartwood – The central core of a tree, which is made up of a layer of dead cells.

June drop – The time during which poorly fertilized fruit falls off the tree. This takes place up to a month after full bloom, and does not necessarily happen in June.

Lateral branch – Branches that grow off the scaffold branches.

Lenticel – Tiny pore in the bark or branches, which allows gas exchange between the plant tissue and the air.

Ovary – The hollow base of the pistil that holds the ovules.

Ovule – Part of the ovary of seed plants that contains the female reproductive cells of the plant.

Phloem – The first layer of cells underneath the tree's bark, where food is transported around the tree.

Photosynthesis – The process by which plants produce food by harnessing sunlight.

Pistil – The female organs of a flower including the stigma, style and ovary.

Rootstock – A tree that will provide the root system and part of the trunk of a grafted tree.

Scaffold branch – Branches that grow out of the tree's trunk.

Stigma – Part of the female reproductive structure of the flower.

Stomata – Holes or pores in the underside of a leaf that absorb carbon dioxide from the air and release water and oxygen back into the air.

Style – A slender part of the flower that leads from the stigma to the ovary.

Suckers – Branches that grow out of the tree's roots which should be pruned off.

Water sprouts – Thin branches that grow vertically off scaffold and lateral branches and that will never produce fruit.

Whip – A one-year-old unbranched fruit tree. It looks like a stick with buds running up its length.

Xylem – The layer of cells underneath the cambium which is made up of sapwood, living cells that transport water up the tree, and heartwood, dead cells that become a part of the dense core of the tree.

Acknowledgements

First and foremost, I want to thank Sherry Firing and Lynn Nicholas, the two amazing women who have worked tirelessly with me to create and maintain Ben Nobleman Park Community Orchard. As our Head Gardener, Sherry has spent hours leading us in our gardening activities, creating harvest festival posters and painting a mural on our orchard shed. As our volunteer coordinator and administrator, Lynn has dedicated hours of her time organizing our stewardship days, working in the park, and keeping our orchard and our group, Growing for Green, running smoothly.

Nothing would have been possible without the more than 20 hands-on volunteers who have poured their love and energy into our park and our orchard through weeding, planting, watering, mulching, helping with festivals and community events, website development and design, writing blogs, copyediting and more. It is your work and care that will help keep our message going and keep our trees strong and productive over the years.

Our city councillor, Joe Mihevc, and his wonderful staff supported us in our dream to create Toronto's first community orchard in a public park. Chris Martin, horticultural supervisor of the City of Toronto's Parks, Forestry and Recreation, always had time for us and helped us develop and carry out our proposal. Other wonderfully supportive Parks, Forestry and Recreation staff included Brian Green, Diane Tomlin and Sandy Straw.

Thank you to our instructors and mentors; Norm Herbert, former orchard manager of E.D. Smith Farms, Ken Slingerland, retired soft fruit expert from the Ontario Ministry of Food and Rural Affairs, and articling agrologist Ray Martinez. They have been there for us in so many ways. Other orchardists who generously shared their knowledge with me are Lorne Jamieson, field manager of Ignatius Farm Jesuit Centre in Guelph, Ontario, Gaye Trombley of Avalon Orchards in Innisfil, Ontario, and Kent Mullinex of The Sharing Farm in Richmond, B.C. And our wonderful fig tree expert, Steve Biggs, not only taught one of our popular workshops but also spent hours poring over this book to offer his suggestions and advice. Thanks as well to my instructor at Ryerson University, ecologist and native tree expert Sam Benvie. He was the first to awaken my passion for trees in general and how much they contribute to our environment.

The funding for our orchard's activities and infrastructure came from generous financial and in-kind contributions from Live Green Toronto, City of Toronto Economic Development, Walmart-Evergreen, Carrot Cache, Fiskars' Tools, Richter's Herbs, Gro-Bark, Green Garage and the Toronto Parks and Trees Foundation. Thanks to their support we have achieved so much in just a few years. Partnering with the Catalyst Centre One-Stop Pop-Ed Shop Worker Co-op has allowed us to accept these grants.

Thank you to Catalyst board members for taking us on!

We are very grateful for our fantastic partners. Not Far from the Tree, founded by Laura Reinsborough, is our harvest partner. Local Enhancement and Appreciation of Forests (LEAF), founded by Janet McKay, has partnered with us for festivals and workshops. Laura and Janet and their teams have promoted our activities, offered us advice and invited us to collaborate on popular events such as the annual Edible Tree Tour. Another wonderful educational partner has been Andrea Dawber and her charity GreenHere. She has offered me advice and support in so many ways.

My inspiration in founding a community orchard was fuelled by the success of other initiatives in North America. In 2010, I was visiting British Columbia and Mary Gazetas, of The Sharing Farm, offered to show me around her group's newly planted orchard in Richmond, B.C. Sadly, Mary died unexpectedly in 2012 and is very much missed. I am grateful to Kimi Hendress, the Sharing Farm's Orchard Manager, for keeping me up to date on their activities. Alison Pultinas, who was involved in Earthworks Boston, gave me a tour of that city's well-established community orchards in 2011. And Bob Baines, of Seattle's Parks Department, dazzled me in 2012 with the blossoming orchards of his city. Seattle's food policy and support for urban growing is an inspiration to cities around the world.

I have yet to visit the orchards of the United Kingdom, but I am grateful to the founders of Common Ground. Their Community Orchard Handbook showed me what was possible when it comes to creating orchard projects in a community. And who gave me that book? Landscape architect Jane Hutton, who volunteered to help us create a design for our orchard to present at community meetings. Without being able to illustrate what we were trying to create, we might not have been given the green light at all. Thank you, Jane!

Today my inspiration comes from the ambitious groups in Toronto that are now following in our footsteps and planting their own orchards. I love working with North York Community House and its Family Tree Project, and with the team at Shoresh, who have recently planted an orchard on donated land at Bela Farm. And I look forward to growing alongside the new orchards of Malvern ANC and the Toronto French School and many other groups.

Thank you as well to the many people who have made creative contributions to our orchard and to our organization, including Tania Janthur, of Bungalow Design, who has created many posters and logos for us over the years. Jack Kirchhoff has copy edited various incarnations of this book and Stephen Grenon has supported us with his photographs, his encouragement and his French-language proficiency.

I want to thank my husband, Cliff Changoor, who is my gardening inspiration. He has been there for me during the good times and stood firmly by my side during the challenging times. When we need heavy work done in the orchard, he is always there, willing to dig out sickly but deeply rooted juniper bushes or shovel huge piles of mulch.

Finally, I want to thank my wonderful parents, Malca and Murray Poizner, who have encouraged me in all my creative initiatives. Thank you for believing in me!

Made in the USA
Charleston, SC
26 February 2015